'There are some books which have the ability to calm, soothe and help you escape the cares of the day. THE WINDING LANE by Derek Tangye is one.' *Daily Mirror*

'The author tells with considerable warmth and understanding of his recent experiences – little charming anecdotes about their donkeys and cats – as well as dips into the past. A real breath of fresh air.' *The Lady*

'An evocative range of home-truths and quips, reminiscence and advice, vision and yet, in a way, rare innocence, another delightful tale comes from the pen of this popular West Cornwall writer ' *The Cornishman*

Also by Derek Tangye in Sphere Books:

COTTAGE ON A CLIFF
SUN ON THE LINTEL
A CAT AFFAIR
SOMEWHERE A CAT IS WAITING
LAMA
DONKEY IN THE MEADOW
THE WAY TO MINACK

The Winding Lane

DEREK TANGYE

Illustrated by Jean Tangye

SPHERE BOOKS LIMITED
30-32 Gray's Inn Road, London WC1X 8JL

First published in Great Britain by Michael Joseph Ltd 1978
Copyright © 1978 by Derek Tangye
First Sphere Books edition 1980
Reprinted 1980, 1981

Printed and bound in Great Britain by
©ollins, Glasgow

To ANDREW and DONALD

ONE

'Where are you going?'

A lovely late May morning, the morning of Fred's birthday. Fred the donkey.

'On a special mission,' I said.

Jeannie laughed. She had just fed Oliver and Ambrose and she was watching them devouring the coley.

'For what purpose?'

'I thought I would go and sit on the rocks and read my diary about the beginning of our life here at Minack.'

I do not understand those who say never look back. By looking back the years are not wasted, and one can place the present in perspective. It is too easy to forget the facts, the incidents, the emotions that have built one's life, long ago reasons which determine today's actions.

'Strange how a girl calling like that can make us think,' Jeannie said.

'One among several people.'

The girl, a young secretary from London, pretty, fair hair to her shoulders, dark blue slacks, a white Shetland polo necked jersey, had provoked me when she walked down the winding lane to the cottage, and asked: 'Have you lost what you once achieved? Have you lost the first vision?'

People who ask direct questions may irritate, but later

you may be grateful to them for stirring the mind. The girl was standing beside the white seat opposite the barn, close to the verbena bush which fills its corner with scent all summer.

'I mean,' the girl went on, 'you have people like me suddenly appearing uninvited, asking you questions, and disturbing your peace, and taking up your time . . . all because of your books about Minack.'

A gull came swooping up the valley from the direction of the sea, and settled on the massive granite chimney, shaking its wings for a second, and looking down on us. It was Philip, easily recognised because he was an old gull. We had other gulls who visited us every day, a pair called Flotsam and Jetsam, a young one called Gus, and one or two others whom I always had difficulty in identifying. For a couple of years there had also been Broadbent the jackdaw, but he had disappeared during the winter, had never come again after a ferocious south westerly gale had blasted the land for twenty-four hours. In his place we now had Ronald the rook, a friendly though cantankerous bird, who regularly arrived at breakfast time, sitting on the apex of the roof, pointing his beak down at us as we sat in the porch, muttering loudly, as if he were saying: 'Give me my bacon rind! Give me my bacon rind!'

'Well,' I replied to the girl, 'I write about reality. I suppose, therefore, it's natural for people to wish to find out whether this reality is true.'

'About what is a dream for many.'

'An unattainable dream for many.'

'Why that?'

'Most people are tied to families, jobs, education for their children, or have grown out of the time to take risks, and however much they would like to start a new kind of life, to try to fulfil a dream, it is impossible for them. And there is the cost. Jeannie and I left London when it was possible to live on very little. To start living a life in the country like ours today costs a small fortune.'

I had picked a tiny sprig of verbena while I was talking, and gave it to her.

'It dries like lavender,' I said, 'and always keeps its scent.'

The girl sniffed it.

'Lovely,' she said, her mind elsewhere.

Then a moment later.

'You still haven't answered my first question.'

'About the first vision?'

'Yes.'

'We haven't a telephone,' I said, making a joke of it.

I had the impression she was upset by my brusqueness I had sounded flippant.

'I suppose you think I shouldn't be asking you these questions, but your books have made me curious to know if you are both still living the kind of life you intended to live when you first arrived.'

Conversation with a stranger can often be less inhibited than with someone one knows.

'People of course have made a difference,' I said, 'but if they take the trouble of tracing our whereabouts, most of them only come because they are on the same wavelength as ourselves. After all, we're difficult to find.'

'No signposts anywhere.'

'And as a result,' I went on, 'we have the experience of meeting all ages, and people from a huge variety of backgrounds, and different countries for that matter, and so we learn a lot.'

The girl was fiddling with her sprig of verbena.

Then again she said: 'You still haven't answered my question.'

'You're very earnest,' I said, making another joke of it. But I added: 'Your question intrigues me. It's just that at the moment I don't know the answer.'

'Are you happy then?'

'Of course we're happy.'

'You see,' she said, 'so many of my generation want to

have a life that fulfils their secret hopes. And we don't know, I at any rate don't know, how we can do so.'

'Nothing new in that. All young generations have been the same.'

We talked for a little while longer. Then she and Jeannie had a word with Oliver, looked for Ambrose but couldn't find him, the girl took a photograph of Penny and Fred, another of Monty's Leap, and said goodbye, and set off up the winding lane, up the hill towards the farm buildings at the top, and the road a mile away.

We watched her go, and I found myself thinking of that first time Jeannie and I came down that winding lane, full also of secret hopes, determined to live off the land and £2.50p a week, and I thought of my diary of that beginning . . .

April 24:

We arrived at midnight on Good Friday April 7, and here it is April 24 and I am beginning my diary. It has been a fortnight of discovery, emotions unfolding, delights which we had imagined but did not know were real. The delight of leisure, for instance. Time to *do* small things without the fear of wasting time. Travelling the day on horseback instead of in a racing car.

Monkey (how did my mother ever get the name of Monkey?) came on April 12 and stayed at the Lamorna Inn for a week. Praise be to the Land Rover. No other vehicle could possibly have coped with the entrance to Minack. It was a wonderful week of happiness. She delighted in buying for us all those domestic things like scrubbing brushes, dust cloths, towels, and mysterious washing powders that make life, in such primitive surroundings, a little less complicated. No one gives of the spirit as she does . . . and together with her presents come her infectious enthusiasm which makes every moment in her company a joy.

Jeannie has just come in to say that Monty has caught

4

a rabbit. His first! He has already settled down, seemingly delighted at exchanging his London life for a country one. He's such a beautiful cat . . . and, poor soul, he had so many hours of his life on his own at Mortlake waiting for us to come home at night. Now he has us all the time to himself.

May 1:
Our potatoes look wonderful. The bitter north wind burnt so many others, but ours were miraculously saved and we now pray for still weather, for in about ten days we should start drawing.

May 4:
Diary of a perfect day—a blue sky and warm breeze—fetch the water from the stream—breakfast of two fresh eggs and coffee—go into the wood looking for stakes for washing line, saw up two small trees—a car arrives with the potato chips, the first car ever to come to Minack!—a man in it, former Jap POW, who said: 'Worse than the Burma Road!'—remove weeds to compost and sprinkle Garotta—take fishing rod to rocks, sea at low tide, then eat a lunch of pâté and biscuits—fish all afternoon, see a baby seal but no fish—return at 4 pm and feed chickens—walk up to the farm for milk—start to break in bog meadow—Frank Hosken, the potato dealer calls, says I should wait till Buryan Feast before starting to draw—have supper of fried corned beef, new potatoes and cabbage—shut the chickens up—play with Monty in the garden—Jean bakes three tarts and twelve tartlets and does some ironing—read 'I Bought a Mountain'—go to bed at 10 pm.

May 10:
A box was delivered at Bill Trevorrow's, the farmer at the top of the hill, by British Railways yesterday. The van obviously couldn't come down to us. It would have

got stuck. Anyhow, we collected the box, hurried back with it to the cottage, and simply couldn't guess what it could be. It was heavy, and it was labelled fragile. How we laughed when we found out what it was! It was a vessel to purify the water we collected from the stream . . . sent by Monkey from Harrods. And of course I realise that this is the result of the tadpole she found in her tea one afternoon. Bless her, she was terribly shaken! And now she goes to all this trouble and expense. It is a splendid looking object, and has the writing on it of Cheavins Saludor (Safe Water) and then underneath, Drinking Water of Absolute Purity. Monkey at any rate won't have a tadpole next time she's here!

May 15:
We started on the potatoes at 4 pm Thursday May 11. Just us two. We have been hard at it ever since and are now utterly, completely exhausted. Jeannie's back is bent double and I am just one ache.

May 19:
We are getting into training and the aches and pains have gone—we have up to now sent away 17 cwt. The crop is excellent. Bill Trevorrow (one of our three farming neighbours, John Ellis and Walter Grose being the other two) said: 'I thought Ellis's samples were good, but they are nothing like these!'—the compliment amazed us, 'like praise from Hugh Wontner' said Jeannie (Sir Hugh Wontner, chairman of the Savoy Hotel, and Jeannie's one time boss)—we have been digging the top cliff and it has been very beautiful there above the sea with the fishing boats sailing to and fro, and the exquisite scent of the bluebells—oh dear, the amount of time spent about disposing of the potatoes! Shall we send to Daniels or to Wespac? Shall we send it by goods or by passenger? John Ellis and ourselves spend hours discussing the whys and wherefores.

June 1:
Disaster! The price has dropped sensationally to 4d (old money)! John came breathlessly into the cottage to tell us

June 12:
Tremendous excitement! Foreign potato imports stopped on the 10th, Lincoln and Pembroke have bad crops, and price has rocketed! . . . 6d a lb at least, perhaps 7d.

June 16:
We've taken £260 on the potatoes and we're thrilled So thrilled in fact that we've taken Tommy Williams on full time (eccentric Tommy lived in a caravan and had helped part time). It's a gamble, but I am seeing into the future. He'll break in a large part of the moorland by next spring, and if we do as well with potatoes next season as this, we're safe.

July 3:
We have 4,000 Governor Herrick violet plants in big field. That ought to bring us in good winter money. Have planted out polyanthus. Reason for their not growing in their boxes was lack of earth. Shall we have arum lilies at the bottom of the bog meadow, or will the drip of rain from the trees spoil the blooms? Shall we try to buy some Sol d'Or on credit, or shall we leave all our land for potatoes?

July 14:
Listened last night to Siegfried from Covent Garden on the radio. We had just had a huge storm, and while the Idyll was being played I saw we were at the parting of the storm. A greenish blue sky to the west, and to the east the lightning lurking with the lights of the fishing boats in Mount's Bay.

July 30:
When staying on holiday with friends in the country, one must never forget that they are working just as *you* would be working had you not gone to stay with them.

August 19:
Here I am on the rocks below Minack with the good intention of catching up on this diary. But how can I write anything when all around is so serenely beautiful? For years my life has been too hectic to *think*. Everything was taken on surface value. Now I am too lazy to think! I am staring blankly at the soothing sea. I have just drawn up the lobster pot, and there are two quite nice crabs. If only we could be totally self-sufficient. Since August 8th, we have had no money except the £100 overdraft guaranteed by Monkey. It was mad of me to take on Tommy full time . . but was it foresight? I hope so.

August 20:
Jeannie sits typing her book late into the night with two candles stuck in bottles beside her on the table. She's decided to call the book *Meet Me at the Savoy*.

September 1:
Saved! Jeannie said this morning as we were about to get up: 'I'm sure you have got an important letter coming in the post.'
The post arrived and with it a letter from my charmer of a 95-year-old cousin Harry enclosing a cheque for £150. Saved from disaster. Tommy's wage assured. We dashed to Lamorna's telephone kiosk and rang Monkey. She was exultant.

September 19:
News from London . . . a gaswork strike, a bus strike, and electricity cuts. So much for city civilisation.
Assorted thoughts from Minack . . . Boswell was a

butterfly who drank too much and was always harassed by debt. He sought out people to pat him on the back and to say how clever he was. Yet he had within him the tenacity and culture to write the *Life*. This achievement gave him no personal satisfaction, for he was still discounted by those, now long forgotten, whose praise he so ardently desired. . . .

An artist has achieved the purpose of his life if he influences, however few in numbers, some people to the good. I have that quiet satisfaction because, though I may not write another book, I *know* that *One King* influenced the unconverted like Shinwell and his colleagues, making them aware that there was more good in the British Empire than bad. And didn't Montgomery make the book a 'must' for all his staff to read after Luneburg Heath?

October 1:
At this stage of our life here, we require: (1) Water . . . the miners digging the well have at last found water, but we will have to buy a pump, buy a tank, and pipe the water down to the cottage. Then we can think about a bath and a lavatory in the cottage. Trouble is that it has cost so much to dig the well that we now haven't the money to bring it to the cottage.

(2) We need a hut to bunch the flowers in, and Tommy must build up the old building below the cottage for a garage.

(3) We need a proper chicken house instead of the small one we brought from Mortlake, and expand the size of the run with wire netting, and we must get 12 chickens on the point of lay.

(4) Rabbits, believe it or not, are cutting the two-inch mesh wire netting round the violets. Am told it isn't unusual, and that it is essential to have one-and-a-half inch mesh.

(5) Sampson Hosking, the violet grower of Lamorna,

advises us to buy fifty-yard rolls of coconut netting as wind protection both for the violets and for the daffodils when they come into flower. Have also to get plenty of posts to hold the netting tight, otherwise the winds blow the bottom of the netting to and fro and this flattens the flowers on either side.

October 17:
As we were warned, red spiders are attacking the Princess of Wales violet plants. The plants look all right one day, but the next they have collapsed in the middle. Such a shame because they have the true violet scent while the Governor Herrick have a lovely colour, but hardly any scent. Tommy Bailey, whose mother keeps the Wink at Lamorna, grows a huge field of violets, and he was giving me tips about them last night:

(1) One should get an average of four boxes per 1,000 plants. Each box containing three dozen bunches, each bunch of eighteen blooms.

(2) When picking them, pick them in bunches as big as your hand can hold and hold them with a rubber band. Pick the leaves later, and if you are short of leaves, use ivy leaves.

(3) Violets feed through their petals, so always keep their petals moist, even when you pack them. Violets will last twice as long if you do this.

November 18:
We have bought a hut, it's a chicken house in fact, and we have put it alongside the end of the cottage. It's twenty feet long and eight feet wide, and we're using it for bunching the violets . . . and Jeannie is using it for writing her book in. I locked her in it this afternoon while I was picking the violets to stop her from joining me. She didn't object! She was glad to be *forced* to get on with writing.

December 10:
To give an idea of violet picking: I went out at 10 am in heavy rain and, bent double, picked incessantly till 1.45 pm. I had ten minutes for lunch, then out into the rain again, this time in the wood to pick ivy leaves. I picked 400, then went over the violets again to pick what I had missed the first time. This evening we went into the hut at 6.45 to bunch, and now it is 9 pm and we have just finished. Marvellously satisfying.

December 18:
Blast it. Here it is Christmas week and we could make a really decent sum out of the violets, but it is bitter cold. Hence there are no blooms and, worse still, there was a storm of hail last night, and this has battered the buds. Not even a bunch to pick for ourselves. Prices will rocket, but we'll have no Christmas bonus.

January 2:
We had a quiet Christmas, and it was very pleasant. On our own all the time except on Christmas Eve when we went to the Tolcarne at Newlyn and then on to the First and Last at Sennen. They both had that atmosphere of an old English pub that people in the cities talk about when they get sentimental. Good fellowship abounded and, during the evening at Sennen, an accordion played, and quite suddenly some men started singing Silent Night.

January 15:
Jeannie is getting on so well with her book that she now is scared because she sees the completion of it in sight! And this means finding a publisher, and then after that whether people will like it. I tell her that any publisher with a grain of intelligence will jump at such a story. [*Meet Me at the Savoy* is still in print but, when the time came, only one publisher, Bill Luscombe, did the jumping.] Irony that she writes about her glamorous days and nights by candlelight in a chicken house.

January 27:

Walked down from the farm just now in a gale . . . chickens huddle beneath the hedges, gulls squatting on the fields, clouds of rain scurrying across Mount's Bay towards the Lizard, and then a flash of sunlight on Minack Wood. To be so happy in such lovely surroundings makes me feel guilty, as if one is not pulling one's weight in life . . . as if one only can fulfil one's destiny by being frustrated, tense, worried.

February 2:

The luck of our coming here is the timing of it. Both of us have satisfied our youthful dreams for fame . . . and how strange it is that the period when a column I once wrote for the *Daily Mirror* was being advertised on London buses, Jeannie should see one such bus passing through Trafalgar Square and say to herself: 'Who is Derek Tangye? Why should he have such publicity?' But both of us have done all the things which ambitious youth aspires after, and thus the restless desire for tinsel pleasures has been killed. Not that either of us has denounced tinsel pleasures. We will enjoy them again I hope, but only as a passing excitement.

March 4:

Sent away one dozen King Alfreds, our very first daffodils we have ever sent away for sale. There is no doubt we should concentrate on King Alfreds. They are such a glorious daffodil. 'The King of Daffs' as someone said. Meanwhile, we have at last finished planting the potatoes . . . three tons of them, and all planted by shovel.

March 13:

A Lizard wind began to blow last night around 5 pm and a storm of rain came too. It has continued on and off for twenty-four hours (mostly on). Just now, after a two or three hour pause in the gale, it suddenly hit the cottage like a slap in the face. Thank heavens the potatoes are not up!

Was up at 6.30, went down to feed the chickens where Hiley the robin greeted me impatiently. He sat as usual on my hand pecking at the crumbs when suddenly another robin appeared. I could sense his excitement as he flew off to a branch a yard away from the other one. There they both perched, stretching their little throats to the sky, but instead of singing, only a cooing sound came from them.

Had breakfast of two boiled eggs and coffee, then went out to pick daffs and when I got round the corner I saw Monty dart towards the discarded potato trays by the garage. Two blackbirds were fighting there. At 7.45 I had enough daffs to start bunching, while Jeannie bunched the few violets we had.

By the time the postman arrived, I had bunched nineteen. A lovely soft morning and once, as I was standing with the daffodils in my hand, I heard a loud purr below me, and there was Monty, sniffing the bunches I had put in a pail of water on the floor. He is usually with us when we bunch, and he likes climbing into the flower boxes.

All morning we bunched, then when we had finished we had lunch of egg sandwiches (praise be to the chickens who are laying over three dozen a week), sitting on the white seat. Then we packed the daffs, and I wrote four letters, and after that drove to Penzance station with them.

Got back at 4.15 with bread for the chickens and fish for Monty . . . but had forgotten to post the letters.

March 21:
Rain, rain, rain. Everyone is worried about the potato prospects. Ground too wet and cold for them to grow. Bill Trevorrow, one of our neighbours, said yesterday there were few stinging nettles growing yet, adding:

'Few stinging nettles mean a bad potato season.' Jeannie and I thereupon hurried down the cliff and were delighted to find splendid looking stinging nettles growing around our meadows!

March 28:
Nothing to do today except enjoy ourselves. The daffs are finished, potatoes down the cliff have broken through the ground and look like small green fists. Nothing we need do about them except hoe the rows, and hope. We are living as peasants in centuries past have lived. We depend on the seasons, depend on finding our pleasure out of natural things around us, and shut our minds to the unsatisfied world outside.

Apri. 1·
We have been here a year! How many people were sure we would be back in London by now! Jeannie's boss at the Savoy expected to see her again within six months, farmers in the neighbourhood, who had seen country enthusiasts without number come and go, also gave us six months. They couldn't understand how Jeannie could stick it. Logic would be on their side. How was it that someone who was at the top of her profession during one of the most dramatic periods of our history could be content to live in a tiny cottage without running water, no electricity, and no telephone?

Nothing of much significance in that diary of the first year. Just enthusiasm, naivety, and hope; and when I finished reading it, I thought again of the girl and her question:

  'Have you lost what you once achieved? . . . Have you lost the first vision?'

TWO

I walked back to the cottage up the cliff path, leaving the sea lapping the rocks, diary under my arm, and as I rounded the bend to the porch, I saw Penny and Fred on the far side of the field, bottoms facing me, their heads nosing the bank beneath the white blossom of a May tree.

Jeannie was sitting in the porch writing a letter.

'Have you given Fred any of his presents while I've been down the cliff?'

'Not yet,' she answered, 'I've been waiting for you,' and then, glancing at me, 'and did your mission come to any conclusions?'

'Hardly conclusions. I'm slow in making up my mind.'

'An understatement!'

True enough. I am inclined to churn over problems. I go on and on discussing a situation which other people might have dismissed in a minute. My behaviour sometimes vexes Jeannie. She is one of those who like to leap over a problem, making a decision by instinct. I too like to use my instinct, rely on it often, but also I like to ally it with a persistent, factual self-questioning. The habit comes from a distinguished member of M.I.5 with whom I once worked. 'Go round and round the facts of a case,' he had said to me, 'and suddenly you will find a chink in the mystery, and everything that puzzled you becomes clear.'

'Anyhow, reading my diary was useful.'

'In what way?'

'It made me realise how easy it is to slide away from truth.'

'I don't understand.'

'I mean it is easy for people to forget their origins and what motivated them in the beginning of their lives. There are obvious examples, like the film star who forgets the time when he was struggling, or the tycoon when he was a clerk, or the Cabinet Minister when he had simple ideals. When they reach their objective, a gloss often covers the truth which at first propelled them. They become puppets in relation to their true selves.'

'You're being too solemn,' said Jeannie.

'The diary has made me solemn.'

'A pity, I'm feeling frivolous.'

'Please, Jeannie, just listen to me for a minute.'

She put down her pen on the table, folded her arms, tried to look solemn, then laughed.

'I'm listening.'

'Be serious.'

'Go ahead.'

'It's just that the diary has set me on my guard, for it is a reflection of the first vision.'

'Nostalgia.'

'No, it isn't that. It's much more fundamental.'

'I'm still listening.'

'It's just that our true base is set around the twenty acres of land, the daffodils we grow, the greenhouses and the tomatoes. We have created all this from barren ground . . . the books come second.'

'But without the books we wouldn't have survived.'

'Of course that's true, but this could deceive us. In the past five years the cost of growing, of wages, have gone up so much that the land cannot now earn the wage of someone working for us. Thus we are on the verge of subsidising a way of life which has little in common with our beginning. That is what I mean by sliding away from truth.'

Jeannie smiled.

'Are you proposing that we should go back to oil lamps and fetching water in a pail?'

'No.'

'Then what are you suggesting? What do you think we can do about it?'

'We have to change direction,' I said.

'What do we do?'

'That's what we will have to decide.'

I left her to finish her letter and went outside to the pocket size front garden, and up to the corner which overlooks the donkey field, and I shouted at the top of my voice: 'Happy birthday, Fred!'

He did not take any notice. Nor did Penny. They had found a delicacy in the bank, a cluster of pink campion perhaps, and no one was going to deter them from having their fill.

'Happy birthday!' I shouted again.

Fred turned his head and looked across the field, just long enough to put me in my place. He was not going to pander to me. If I wished to behave foolishly, let me do so. He was occupied. He would continue to nose out the delicacy in the bank.

I sympathised with him in theory. I do not enjoy my own birthdays. I do not want to be reminded that the years are passing. I am not in tune with those who proudly announce, like a batsman totting up a score . . . 'I am forty, I am fifty, I am sixty' . . . and then hasten out to celebrate. It is as if nothing has been achieved in their lives except age.

For I prefer to believe that age is an attitude of mind, and that the young can be old, and the old young. Maybe those who have no children have an advantage in thinking this way. They are not made aware of the generation gap in the manner that parents are made aware. They can behave towards children as equals because they have no personal responsibility towards them, and so, as with grown ups, their relationship with children depends upon sharing a common wavelength; and one can have a common wavelength with a six-year-old.

There was a six-year-old who came to Minack with her mother to whom we showed Oliver and Ambrose, and to whom we introduced Fred and Penny (she had a ride on Penny); and at the end of her visit she solemnly called me aside, then proceeded to present me with 2p. Her mother was out of sight, and when I told her she said: 'All Josephine's worldly goods.' I took the coin and buried it in a shallow bed of earth underneath a large rock, and told Josephine, earnest face looking up at me: 'Come back in twenty years and it will still be here where we have buried it . . . and we will call this Josephine's corner.'

A few weeks later, however, I had a rebuff. A small boy came down the winding lane one day in the company of his parents, and I immediately asked him whether he would like to see the donkeys. He walked silently with me up to the gate where the donkeys were standing and, as a way of making conversation, I asked him whether he had ever had a ride on a donkey.

'No.'

'Do you like donkeys?' I asked.

'No.'

'Have you ever seen donkeys before?'

'No.'

'Would you like to give the donkeys a biscuit?'

'No.'

'Would you like to stroke their noses?'

'No.'

At that I admitted defeat.

Fred's birthday, however, is a ritual. He had arrived at

Minack, as some will remember, by mistake. Jeannie and I were enjoying an evening at a pub near Redruth when the publican persuaded Jeannie to buy a forlorn looking donkey which he kept in a field (now bordered by a dual carriageway) near the pub; and so, at the end of the evening, I found myself returning to Minack with a black donkey in the well of the Land Rover, her head resting on my shoulder as I drove, trustfully hoping she was going to a home where she would be loved for the rest of her life. This was Penny; and a month later, in a sloping field overlooking Mount's Bay through which the Coastal Path now passes, and known by ourselves as Fred's field, Fred was born.

'You're going to have two donkeys and not one,' the publican had said as we manoeuvred Penny that evening into the Land Rover, 'you've got a bargain.'

Penny came from the hills of Connemara, or so we believed, and wanted to believe. Naturally we were inquisitive about her past, and we set out to discover it; and though the trail was to prove a vague one, there were certain aspects of her story we could establish.

We traced, for instance, the dealer who had bought her at an auction in Exeter market. He came from a village between Truro and Redruth, and he told us that there had been a batch of donkeys at the auction, and the sales catalogue had said they had been shipped from Connemara. He went on to say that he had had no intention of buying a donkey that day, but he had been so struck by Penny's appearance, her beautiful head and her fine black coat, and her aristocratic manner as she stood waiting for the auction to begin, that he found himself bidding for her; and to his surprise buying her.

He did not keep her long. He sold her to a corn merchant in Camelford, who kept her in a field near his house close to the main road that leads to Bude. Jeannie and I have made a pilgrimage to this field, and we have seen the hedges beside which Penny sheltered, and the gate over which she watched the traffic passing by. At this time, she was already carrying Fred; and it was at this time that she had a moment of glory when she took part in the Camelford Summer Parade, pulling a decorated cart, shining harness adorning her, a brass band playing, shouts from the crowd, and the children running beside her.

The corn merchant in due course sold her because he found her so sad. She depressed him by her lassitude, by the manner in which she used to position herself, bottom to hedge, mournfully allowing the hours to pass by. Had she not so depressed the corn merchant, she would never have come to Minack . . . for the corn merchant sold her to the publican, who sold her to us.

But this attitude of Penny we came to know ourselves. She always seemed to be looking into the distance, far, far away, as if there were some magical time when she was a young donkey that she yearned to experience again; and, in a way, we felt thwarted by her attitude. *What* was she yearning for? *Where* exactly was she born? Where was the colleen now who first loved her? What were the circumstances which set her off on the long journey from Connemara via Dublin, Fishguard, Exeter to Camelford, Redruth to Minack? *Why* did somebody in Connemara decide to sell her? Maddening that we will never know, maddening that all the hours we have spent holding her head, letting her nuzzle us, talking nonsense to her, receiving comfort from her, caring for her in a thousand ways . . . yet all the years before she came to England will remain a vacuum.

How many years, however, were there? The publican had said she was four years old. A vet confirmed this, but it is difficult to tell the age of a donkey in certain circumstances. Perhaps, therefore, she was many years older. For all I know she may have been twenty or thirty, not four, when she came to Minack. For all I know, her Connemara owner sold her because her working life was over. Anyhow, if that were true, she came to the right place. There was no work for her to do here. Her only job was to give pleasure.

Fred's birthday ritual began as a result of what happened on his first birthday. Soon after breakfast on that day a large envelope was delivered at the cottage by two emissaries from St Buryan School, the local school; and inside the envelope, to our surprise, was an array of gaily coloured crayon pictures of Fred in happy situations. Fred with carrots dangling in front of his nose; Fred in a halo of apples; Fred with Penny beside him, and Penny apparently presenting him with a large slab of chocolate; and of course each picture was accompanied by its message . . . 'Happy birthday Freddie' . . . 'Have a good time dear Fred' . . . and all signed by the girls and boys of St Buryan School, who have now long ago grown up.

That was the beginning of Fred's first birthday; and it was followed in the afternoon by a party in the field above the cottage with a cake and one candle, and ice creams; and the children vieing with each other to gain the favour of Fred's attention, while Penny sedately played nanna to them all, walking up and down the field with one, sometimes two on her back, surrounded by others calling out: 'Can I have a ride? Can I? Can I?'

There was not another party for five years, but the birthday crayon coloured good wishes continued to arrive and, on Fred's behalf, we arranged for ice creams to be given to the children on the day; and then there was a party three years after the second one when a BBC television team filmed the party, and there was Fred surrounded by a swarm of his guests, revelling in the attention, sharing with Penny a special cake that was decorated with marzipan carrots and marzipan apples. He has had no party since. There could not be another to equal the last one. But he still has his birthday cards. The children of St Buryan no longer send them, quite understandably, because Fred is older than most of them; and

23

instead he has others, more elaborate than the crayon coloured pictures, and sent to him by those who have read his story, or visited him at Minack. Sometimes parcels arrive too . . . carrots inevitably, and apples, and potato crisps, and chocolate digestive biscuits. And on this occasion, this occasion when I was calling to him across the field, there were twenty-five birthday cards and four parcels.

I wonder sometimes about this fascination for donkeys. Perhaps it is just another example of the sentimental love for animals from which so many people draw comfort as an antidote to modern living. Perhaps it is because they are remote creatures available only for a few lucky enough to have a paddock large enough for a donkey to graze. Perhaps it is because they are a reminder of past holidays with donkey rides on the sands. Perhaps it is because they have been glamorised by their history of buffeting and ill treatment throughout the world, and therefore, they are an emblem to many people of the downtrodden. Perhaps the immortal lines of G. K. Chesterton have much to do with the donkey spell. Perhaps the Bible. The donkey is mentioned more often in the Bible than any other animal; and of course the heart of its biblical association is the story of Christ riding a donkey into Jerusalem on Palm Sunday.

'Rejoice greatly, O daughter of Zion' had foretold Zacharia. 'Shout, O daughter of Jerusalem: behold thy king cometh unto thee, he is just and having salvation, lowly and riding upon an ass and upon a colt, the foal of an ass.'

Yet why should the word ass become, in due course, a word of insult? Was it Shakespeare's fault by use of Bottom's antics in Midsummer's Night Dream? . . . 'don't be an ass' . . . 'stupid ass' . . . 'silly ass' . . . all these terms of derision are heaped upon an animal which is among the most intelligent. In ancient times there was no such derision. A donkey was considered superior to a horse, and a king or chieftain on great occasions always rode on a donkey. Such a tradition led Jesus on a donkey into Jerusalem.

'Fred!' I shouted once more across the field, and then gave up. He may have been an intelligent donkey, but he was also an obstinate one.

'He has no interest in his birthday,' I said to Jeannie, reacting like a small boy who had been thwarted.

'He'll change his mind later, you'll see.'

She had moved from the porch into the tiny kitchen where she was checking the bread baking in the oven. We had recently changed our electric cooker for a calor gas cooker. It was fed from two gas cylinders hidden from sight behind a stone wall outside the cottage and, as soon as one cylinder was empty, the other one was automatically switched on, and a delivery service then replaced the empty one. It was an admirable cooker, we were independent of electricity cuts, it was cheaper, and the gas flame was more gentle for cooking. The only snag was that I am suspicious of gas; and I have particular cause to be after two scaring experiences with a gas poker.

I had used a gas poker for years to light the fire without problems arising. The time came, however, when the poker wore out and had to be replaced by a new one. All seemed normal when I carried the small gas cylinder to which the new poker was attached up to the fireplace. There I lit a match, loosened the tap on the cylinder, then held the match against the poker.

Both poker and cylinder promptly went up in flames.

I yelled to Jeannie who was in the bedroom, and she rushed to my aid by opening the front door, then the porch door while I, my hand among the flames and holding the cylinder handle, half dragged, half carried the cylinder until I was able to fling it into the garden where it continued to blaze like a petrol bomb. My hand was singed, but fortunately there was no serious hurt. Naturally I was puzzled as to what had happened, but I was inclined to blame myself. I thought, perhaps, I had not fastened the connections tight enough.

Next day I obtained another poker, another cylinder, taking the precaution of having the poker fixed to the cylinder by the suppliers; and that evening I approached the fireplace again. I double checked the connections, gingerly held the poker in front of me, lit a match, half turned the tap and . . . whoosh! Cylinder and poker were in flames again; and once again it was miraculous that I got them outside without setting the cottage on fire or harm to myself.

What had gone wrong? Years of using a gas poker without trouble, and now twice an experience which, if it had happened to Jeannie on her own, or to someone without the strength to carry the cylinder away with speed, would have resulted in a disaster. There was also an aspect, apart from a personal one. Other people might be running the same risk. I visioned a rash of exploding gas pokers.

Thus I alerted the Penzance Fire Brigade, then the suppliers; and both reacted with anxiety. The potential danger was enormous, not just in Cornwall, but wherever gas pokers were in use. So why had my gas poker behaved so out of character?

A few days later a representative of the makers arrived at the door, took notes, looked serious, but said nothing except that a thorough investigation would be made; and in due course I heard the result of the investigation.

Modern production methods had substituted a plastic washer for a rubber one at the connection point between poker and cylinder; and this failed to seal the gas once the tap was turned. Thus gas was in the air when I lit the match, and hence the flames. All is well now. The plastic washers were withdrawn, so also the pokers which had been fitted with them; and I have heard of no trouble since.

We had first called Penny Jenny, after a friend of ours called Jenny Napper; and Fred was called after her husband, Fred Napper. In those days we were so ignorant of the donkey world that we did not know that all female donkeys are jennys in donkey language; and it was for this reason, after we had learnt about it, that Jenny became Penny.

Fred and Jenny Napper were old enough to be our parents. They lived in a rambling house with a large sloping garden overlooking the valley of Lamorna. It is a lovely wooded valley, the valley of Lamorna; and though some may say it is being spoilt, there is still none of the harsh exploitation from which many other beauty spots are suffering. Trees hide new bungalows, the steepness of the land prevents major development. It is a valley of compromise. The necessity of financial survival forces people to sell land they own, but the planners, so far, have prevented ugliness. Down in the cove there is a car park, of course, but the cost of the fee is mitigated by the welcome the car owner receives from the gentleman in charge . . . Garston Barnes, ex-farmer, ex-fisherman, chiselled sun-burnt face like that of a pirate, who accepts the fee with such a pleasant air, gives advice of where to go and what to do with such a natural desire to help, that only the churlish grumble as to why they should pay a fee at all.

Yet at Lamorna there would be no car park, no harbour wall for that matter, no place for local fishermen to keep their boats, had it not been for the enterprise of John Daniel, one time Penzance ice-cream merchant, now local councillor and county councillor, who bought most of the cove when it was becoming derelict and the harbour wall collapsing. He is very Cornish. Meet him outside his café, granite built beside the quay and, whoever you are, he will say: 'Hello, m'handsome' or 'How are you doing, m'dear?'

John Daniel is an institution of Lamorna valley, like Garston Barnes. So too is Sampson Hosking, whose family has rented the land on one side of the valley for generations. Jeannie and I owe a great deal to Sampson Hosking.

He is one of those people who, selflessly, want to help others. He is also a musician and well known for his work, first with the Mousehole choir, now with the Lamorna choir, which he created. We met him when we first came to Lamorna on a holiday; and at a time when I was enduring the illusion that I could make a fortune out of a 'take away' restaurant at Kingston upon Thames in Surrey. Sampson Hosking was the most famous violet grower in West Cornwall at that time; and he sent me each week a box of Governor Herrick violets, from which, when my fancy took me, I gave a bunch to a favourite customer. My 'take away' restaurant failed because it was before its time; and then the sweet violets of Sampson Hosking failed. Costs out-stripped the returns; and though Sampson and his wife Janie, and Estelle, his daughter, a famous flower arranger, and her husband, still grow violets, they grow very few in comparison with the time when Jeannie and I first came to Lamorna when, on still days in November, the valley was touched with the scent of violets.

The Hoskings live in the prettiest part of Lamorna . . . past The Wink, the village inn which is renowned for its display of ship relics collected by the landlord, past the village shop where the Murleys reign and where Mrs Murley thrusts carrots at the donkeys when we come on our occasional visits, past two cottages and across the bridge over the bustling Lamorna stream to where a giant water wheel stands, a wheel which is still in working order; a quiet world of tall trees and old buildings, and ghosts of men and women carrying baskets of daffodils, and violets, and anemones to the packing sheds from the fields leaning above the valley. These fields you can see from the Napper house; and in the spring the fields startle you, a landscape of golden yellow against the leafless trees of the valley woods.

Fred and Jenny Napper were a couple with old world manners and modern minds. Fred Napper was a retired

28

leather merchant, who once had also farmed in Sussex. He found special pleasure in possessing fine china, fine glass, and fine wine. He was always courteous, and he was wise. Many a time did I ask him for advice when Jeannie and I were struggling at Minack, when I was bewildered what to do if we were to survive; and he would, by his advice, help to counter my panic. I remember one day when, it seemed, there was no alternative for Jeannie and me but to pack up and return to London, that he quoted the three famous lines:

> Money lost little lost
> Honour lost much lost
> Courage lost all lost.

He had opened a bottle of wine, and his gnarled, arthritic hand raised his glass to mine. 'Always remember that last line. It's helped a lot of people much worse off than you out of trouble.'

Each possessed ancient cars and continued to drive them long after, one would have thought, it would have been more suitable for them to possess a small modern one. Fred had an Alvis open sports car. Jenny had her own sports car, a yellow one, an Hispano Suiza I believe it was, and I have often seen her incongruously clad in early twentieth-century motoring clothes, gripping the wheel, wind or rain no matter, driving to Penzance. They both had a gusto for life.

Jenny was also impulsive. Her life was governed by hunches and a ceaseless desire to be kind to everyone. She would, for instance, disturb some of her closer friends by encouraging total strangers to visit her. She would be in Penzance walking up Market Jew Street, and she might drop a glove, and someone would run after her and give it back to her. 'Oh, you *are* nice,' she would say. 'Now I'll tell you where I live . . . and you must come out to see me.' Or she might startle a stranger who was standing beside her in a shop by saying: 'My dear, you're in trouble

29

. . . I can see it in your eyes. What's wrong?' And the stranger would suddenly find herself free to unburden herself.

She had old-fashioned standards. She had lived through an age when manners mattered more than affluence. She was courteous to everyone. In her home she refused to accept the value of modern labour saving devices. She never possessed a fridge because she considered it took away the true taste of food. She preferred an old fashioned larder, facing north. She liked to bathe, and this was a ceremony she took great pains about. On waking up in the morning, she would observe the haze over the valley, and decide the day was going to be a hot one. She would leisurely dress herself (summer or winter, she always wore a flowered frock), see that her hair was arranged just as she wanted ('Never, dear,' she said to Jeannie, 'take yourself for granted'), and then set off for the rock pools between Lamorna and Carn Barges, carrying an ancient black bathing dress and a cap. Jenny was one of those who relished the gentler aspects of living and, by doing so, gave much in spirit to other people.

Fred died before Jenny; and, during his last illness, Jeannie once a week shopped for them both, and then took their goods out to the rambling house, and Fred would call from his room to see her; and, as she left, Jenny impulsively would take some exotic purchase that Jeannie had made for her, like a fresh pineapple, and thrust it into Jeannie's hands. 'Give it to Derek,' she would say. We regularly called on her after Fred died, and often we walked the donkeys to see her, and the last time we did so she gave Penny a fat kiss on her nose. It was a significant moment in view of what was to happen.

'Bread's done to perfection,' I heard Jeannie call from the kitchen, and she came out carrying four hot, fragrant loaves. 'That'll be enough for a week,' she added.

At that moment there was a bellow from the field. Fred was ready for his presents.

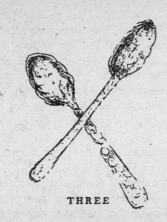

THREE

The swallows were late in coming to Minack that year.
I had first seen a pair early in April, skimming the low
stone walls between Morvah and Zennor, then a couple of
weeks later a scattered few flew over Minack and, all
through May, there was an increasing number of groups
flying east along the cliff, but none of them showed signs
of wishing to stay around Minack.

I was not unduly upset by this. For three successive
years we had had swallows nesting in the barn. Then
there were none for a year. Then, once again, there was a
nest, and then last year they again failed to arrive.
Swallows are reputed to bring luck to the home where they
nest, but I had not noted any special change in our luck,
one way or another, whether they were with us or absent.

A few days after Fred's birthday, however, I was
unlatching the gate opposite the barn on my way towards
the cliffs when I saw a swallow sweep out of the barn
doorway, followed by another one. The sight of them did
not necessarily mean that they had decided to nest there.
In past years I had watched pairs making an inspection,
then, having found the site unsuitable, flying away. And,
for several reasons, the site *was* unsuitable.

The donkeys, for instance, presented a problem. Penny
and Fred, in hot weather, liked to shelter in the shade of

the barn away from the flies. It is a small barn with feet thick granite walls, a cobbled floor, two small windows facing the lane, the door opening on a little yard and facing the sea; and there is a gap at one end of the yard which leads to the stable meadow, and opposite the gap is a white wooden fence with a small gate that opens up on a space covered with grey stone chippings where a visitor parks his car.

The barn is very old, and there is a record of it standing there in 1704. One half has an attic with a floor of ancient planks where once upon a time seed potatoes were 'shot', and which is now a repository of all those assorted articles which I cannot make up my mind whether to keep or not. Look upwards from the cobbled floor in the other half, and you see the cobwebbed roof of the barn and, though the beams look solid, the battens holding the slates remind you of driftwood on the seashore, so broken and splintered are they, and you wonder how the roof stays intact when the gales blow. Up there, close to the broken battens, wedged beside the beams, are three past mud nests of swallows; and there are two more on a ledge directly beneath the planks of the attic. These two caused me much concern when they were built, for the ledge is so low that the donkeys merely had to lift their heads and knock them to pieces had they so wished.

Thus I doubted the wisdom of swallows nesting in the barn . . . the top nests surrounded by shaky supports, the lower ones threatened by a donkey's nose. Jeannie was sure that fate would see that all would be well, but I didn't share her view. I may have rejoiced at the sight of the swallows gyrating in the sky, and dashing in and out of the door at high speed, but I was always apprehensive. I was thankful when the summer ended and the swallows had flown away, and no harm had come to them.

So, when that day I saw the swallows fly out of the barn door, one part of me wanted to hurry back and tell Jeannie, while another part of me had a weary sense of apprehension. If they nest, this part of me said, I will have to be on guard throughout the summer. I will have to watch the donkeys, I will have to worry about the condition of the battens, and when visitors arrive and park their cars by the white fence, I will quickly have to manoeuvre them away so that the swallows are not disturbed by their presence . . . and I will also have to be concerned about the attitude of the cats. Oliver the black double of Lama. Ambrose the ginger double of Monty; Monty, the cat who changed me from a cat hater into a cat lover.

Neither Monty nor Lama had been bird chasers. Nor, for that matter, was Oliver a bird chaser, although I once knew him catch a dunnock, that brown little bird which scurries around the garden resembling a mouse. Ambrose, on the other hand, when he was very young, *did* catch birds. I used to see him sitting on an outhouse window-sill waiting for the wrens in winter to come at dusk to their roosting quarters in a hole above the window; and I would run towards him shouting like a hyena frightening him away. He seemed to have learnt his lesson. I had not seen him catch a bird for a long time.

Yet I cannot take this apparent good nature for granted. He may not be a bird chaser, nor Oliver, but if either of them sees a bird on the ground, and it moves, they might easily pounce upon it, as they might pounce out of fun on a fluttering leaf.

I am always anxious, for instance, about Charlie. Charlie the chaffinch, successor to a previous Charlie, has been in residence at Minack for six years or more, and he is as tame as a budgerigar, except he is not in a cage, and the land around Minack is his kingdom. In autumn and winter he is a dull coloured little bird, but in summer he is exotic with his resplendent slate blue head and brilliant white wing feathers; and while in winter he is quiet, in summer he is full of jauntiness . . . and self-confidence. If it is a sunny morning and we are having breakfast on the bridge, the bridge so-called because from it we look out across the sea of Mount's Bay as if we were on the bridge of a ship, he will appear on the glass top of the garden table while I am enjoying my eggs and bacon, and demand to have a peck at it. Or he will sit on a rock near by me and shout his: 'Cheep, cheep!' at me, waiting for a chance to have a bite at the butter on the table; and, after a while, I will say impatiently: 'Shut your beak, Charlie!' Charlie, by his attitude that all the world is safe for him, causes me concern when Oliver and Ambrose are in the neighbourhood.

The threat posed to the swallows, however, by Oliver and Ambrose was twofold. It was possible, for instance, for them to climb up into the attic, then along one of the beams to where the swallows had built their mud nest, or if the nest were on the ledge below the planks of the attic, it was possible that they could squeeze along the ledge. Either possibility was remote, but I had to consider them. Thus to deal with the first threat I had to block any cat route to the attic, and to deal with the second I had to block the openings to the ledge. My swallow neurosis, therefore, my fear as to what the donkeys might do and what the cats might do, made me hope whenever I watched the swallows making their inspection that they might sense the possible dangers and fly away elsewhere. This time, the pair I had seen decided to stay; and within a month they were in trouble. Their choice of site for the first nest was up against a rafter, adding mud to one which had been built in a previous year. The mixture wasn't solid enough. One night, a month later, there was a gale accompanied by heavy rain . . . and all that was left of the nest the following morning was a crumble of dry mud, and a single broken egg on the cobble stone floor of the barn. Within a week they began to build another. This time on the ledge directly beneath the planks of the attic, a couple of feet away from the old nest of Pip and Squeak and Wilfred, about whom I wrote in *A Cornish Summer*.

Meanwhile, every day we continued to discuss our future. One late June morning we were sipping coffee, eating coconut cake, on the bridge. A warm morning . . the scent of honeysuckle climbing the wall nearby, the heavy blossom of the May tree in the lane beginning to show a shade of pink, a blackbird singing in a tree by Monty's Leap, an unidentifiable green insect settling on my hand, Flotsam and Jetsam the gulls looking down on us from the old stone chimney, Charlie cheeping, a cuckoo calling on Carn Barges, the castle-like rocks overhanging the sea, two cabbage whites chasing each other, the first white flowers on the elder tree opposite the barn; and in and out of the barn, flashing blue-black darts, were the swallows.

'Geoffrey has picked twenty chips this morning,' I said to Jeannie.

Geoffrey had been with us since the days of Jane of *A Drake at the Door*, then he went elsewhere for a while, and returned to Minack after we had given up early potatoes, and were concentrating instead on daffodils and tomatoes. We had three thousand tomato plants in heated greenhouses.

'They're beginning to move,' I added.

'Not fast enough,' answered Jeannie.

June is the month when one depends on good prices and a quickly maturing crop. By July prices begin to dip. By August, when the coldhouse tomatoes begin to flood the market, prices are usually on the floor.

'Geoffrey is a bit edgy.'

'Why?' she asked.

'I don't blame him. It is because he realises his future may depend on the tomato crop . . . it's the uncertainty which is upsetting him.'

'The trouble is,' said Jeannie, 'that when he first came here the fact of being a good shoveller was the passport to success.'

True enough. The man who was able to use the long

Cornish shovel with speed and efficiency, turning ground, planting potatoes, digging them, was a prize among men. Geoffrey was one of them. But gradually scientific methods of growing began to develop, and skill was required to make use of the methods, and shovel men like Geoffrey had difficulty in adjusting. I would try to encourage him by arranging for him to go to one of the admirable demonstrations organised by the Ministry of Agriculture; and when I saw him the next day I would ask how he had got on.

'A good tea,' he would reply, smiling.

The relationship between boss and employee becomes ever more complicated; and although one may grumble about union power and government cossetting, this state of affairs is an inevitable result of boss ruthlessness in the past.

My grandfather Sir Richard Tangye was a boss, but he was far from being a ruthless one. He set off from the village shop in Illogan near Redruth with his brothers to found the great engineering firm of Tangyes in Birmingham; and he was to become known as one of the great Liberal industrial reformers of the late nineteenth century. He was heartily disliked by other bosses because of the reforms in working conditions that he introduced, and for his philosophy that the worker had as much right to civilised living as more fortunate people.

I do not believe, however, that he would ever have accepted the modern worship of equality. Somebody has to lead, the great majority has to follow. Some have the brains, the capacity for hard work in excess of normal requirements, the readiness to take risks, the flair for exploiting opportunities, while others are born with a dunce's cap or are content to tick their lives away without wishing to accept responsibility or are blind to the opportunities which are presented to them.

My grandfather was a natural leader. He did not see the acquisition of money as an end in itself, nor as a means to live extravagantly. He believed that money should be used to broaden the horizons of the poor, but not to delude them into thinking that money came to their door-step by right. After all, he was a living example of this philosophy. From his very humble beginnings he became a great industrialist, taught himself to become the greatest Cromwellian expert of his day possessing the finest Cromwellian collection in the country, which was later given to the nation. He taught himself also to be an authority on Wedgwood china, and, when offered a peer-age, declined it, and only accepted a knighthood because he considered it a tribute to his workforce who had made Tangye engineering products famous throughout the world. Liberal minded though he was, I do not see him fitting into the mood of today.

There are some echoes of him in me, but I do not possess his toughness. My grandfather would make a decision and would expect the decision to be successfully carried out by those designated to do so. I, on the other hand, am inclined to waffle. The fact is that I am seldom positively sure that the decision I have come to is the correct one. Hence I am inhibited against giving orders. I often failed in my relationship with Geoffrey by asking him what *he* thought instead of telling him what *I* thought. It was a subconscious twist in my character that seemed to believe it was wrong to give orders to another human being.

Geoffrey sensed this weakness on my part and thus when I asked him to do something, or whether he thought a certain action should be taken, he, with no wish to carry the responsibility of the decision himself, would respond with the phrase 'up to you'.

I, therefore, might ask whether a field was ready to be ploughed, instead of telling him to plough it, and he would answer: 'Up to you.' Or, on the occasion when he had picked the twenty chips of tomatoes, I should not have asked him whether he was going to take them into Penzance in the afternoon or morning because I should have known that I would receive the inevitable reply: 'Up to you.'

An unfortunate aspect of these interchanges was the failure to make him feel he was a partner. I yearned for him to take charge of the day to day business of the market garden while I pursued my other affairs. He did not want such responsibility. He was one of the legion who wanted to be led; and as the wages crept up year after year, and so too the general expenses, I began to feel I was in pawn to him. He was as honest as could be, but he was causing me strain. The boss, in fact, was losing the purpose of being the boss. The rewards were fast disappearing. Like others in similar situations, in other small businesses, I was imprisoned in numerous government regulations, and the ever increasing enforced wages which bore no relation to the turnover or income that could be obtained from the business. Each day, therefore, was bringing increasing disenchantment. I was losing my freedom.

My mood had conveyed itself to Geoffrey, and this was the cause of his being edgy.

'He wants a couple of hours off,' I said to Jeannie.

'But that's the second couple of hours this week!'

'It's some private business.'

'This is all becoming such a burden,' said Jeannie.

'It's government regulations as well. Some of these regulations scare me. I can't see how the small business man can cope with them.'

'If Geoffrey went,' said Jeannie, 'he would have his redundancy money. Have you ever worked out what it would be?'

'Around £500, and we get half of that back.'

'Sooner or later we'll have to face up to it . . . if we want to be free of the strain.'

'We would give him plenty of notice,' I said, 'three months perhaps. It would give him enough time to find the right kind of job.'

'We must do that.'

'We'll have to think about it more,' I said, 'we have to change direction that's true, but let's do it carefully. We have to work out what it would entail if he left.'

Three thousand tomato plants take a lot of time to look after. The cycle of growing them began in the autumn after the old plants had been pulled up and carried away. First the ground was rotovated, watered and sterilised with a powder which was also rotovated into the soil, and left there, the greenhouse shut up, for six weeks. Then, in the New Year, after the powder had performed its task of destroying the soil pests and fungi, the ground was rotovated again along with the appropriate amount of tomato base fertiliser. Now came an interval while we dealt with the invasion of daffodils. In the middle of March the tomato plants were delivered, and a hectic period of planting took place, particularly hectic if the daffodil season was a late one. For a while, after planting, the tomato plants demanded nothing of us as they settled their roots into the soil but, as soon as they started to grow, stringing had to begin; and attaching three thousand strings to an overhead wire and tieing each one to a plant was a formidably slow task.

From now on, for the following five months, the plants had to be cherished in numerous ways. Soon the wearisome task of pinching out began, pinching out the shoots that grew from the joints of the plant, shoots which, if left to grow, would take away strength from the main stem. It was a dirty task too, a dirty green task, because the juice stained your fingers, stained also the clothes you wore as you moved among the plants. No machine could do the job. Until horticultural researchers develop a tomato plant which doesn't sprout shoots, this work will always be performed by hand labour.

Watering and feeding, however, was done automatically, although in our case, at this period I am writing about, we had run into trouble. The water was pumped from our own small reservoir to the greenhouses via a specially designed tank which stored the liquid manure which we always made ourselves as it was very much cheaper to do so than to buy the ready made manure; and on the tank was a dial which you turned to obtain the appropriate strength of feeding mixture. This operated very successfully. Unfortunately, it was not so successful in reaching the plants because of the poor condition of the rubber tubing which ran along the base of each row with a nozzle for each plant. The tubing had been in use for years and, in numerous places, the rubber had begun to perish; and so instead of each plant receiving its quota of water and feed, many received none at all. Leaks in the tubing were everywhere; and Geoffrey spent many hours of his time trying to plug them. Of course, I should have bought new equipment, but I did not do so because I did not believe that the likely returns merited the very considerable capital expenditure required.

Such tomato tasks, if Geoffrey left, would have to be done by myself. I would also have to deal with the temperamental heating installations which sometimes, for no apparent reason, cut out during the night. On the other hand, I had experience in all these matters because at weekends, when Geoffrey was at home, I was always in charge; and I had learnt to coax the heaters back into operation, and to cope with the rubber tubing. I did, however, have a feeling of frustration. I had better things to do.

Thus maintenance would be a time consuming problem if Geoffrey left. He was good at maintenance. He had inherited from his father, a craftsman carpenter who had built our porch, the ability to use wood; and whenever it was necessary he was able to act as a carpenter. The wooden roof of what serves as a garage was repaired by Geoffrey. He could make a bench for us to sit on in the garden. He repaired gates, and he was able to instal the packing benches where we bunch and pack in the small greenhouse. He painted when necessary, and he had the time to tinker with machines like the mower or the rotovator when they refused to start. He did not, however, have the time to maintain the greenhouses, or more accurately I did not tell him to make the time. He would always refit a broken glass pane, but I never told him to paint the wooden frames of the greenhouses with wood preservative. It was very foolish of me, and I increasingly regret my omission.

I particularly regret my failure to take proper care of the Orlyt, the twenty feet wide and one hundred feet long greenhouse which stands below the cottage. The frames are of cedar wood, and I was informed when I chose it that cedar wood lasted for ever; and I was lulled, incredibly, into never inspecting the condition of the wood as the years went by. Nor, for that matter, and equally incredibly, did I ever discover until recently that the erectors of the Orlyt had fixed the far end of the greenhouse fourteen inches out of true. Nothing I can do about that now, but I am still wondering what to do about the wood. Parts of it are rotting, and I have a nightmare that one day the greenhouse will resemble a block of greenhouses that we used to observe at Poljigga on the way to Land's End.

These had been built towards the end of the last century by a carpenter and his family and, for a while, they became famous for the grapes that were grown there. Holiday visitors in horse drawn carriages used to call there for the grapes, and one summer when the grapes were in specially fine condition a basket of them was despatched to Queen Victoria at Balmoral; and it was reported that she was delighted with them and, as a result, the carpenter became locally known as the King of Grapes. Alas, as the years went by, the gales battered the greenhouses, the wood rotted, the glass smashed, and only a derelict shell remained to remind passers-by of where the famous grapes once grew.

The Orlyt had a special significance for us; a sentimental

value because it was the first greenhouse we possessed, decided upon after much earnest discussion, bought with borrowed money, and looked upon by us after its installation as a gateway to an *el dorado*. Jane was with us then, Jane with the flowing blonde hair, Jane who at the age of fifteen said she wasn't going to have any more of school and that she was going to work for us, and who used to walk barefooted across the fields from the cottage on the cliff a mile or so away, where she lived with her mother and a sheep, a dog, two cats and a parrot. Only yesterday, when a young art student came down the lane with her husband, one of the questions she asked was what happened to Jane and what happened to the cottage where she lived.

'The middle one, wasn't it?' the girl said, as if she had been there.

I explained to her then that after Jane and her mother left, the three cottages were bought and turned into a luxury house. As for Jane herself, I said, she lived for a while on Bryher in the Scilly Isles, and now had moved to Tresco with her two children, one of whom, Sylvia, was our god-daughter, and where her husband now worked in Tresco Gardens.

'Where was it,' the girl then asked, 'that Jane kept her flowers the night of the storm before she won the prize at the Flower Show?'

I showed her the corner of the Orlyt where Jane had kept her Carbineer daffodils. She had brought them over from the Scillies, and on the night she arrived one of the most violent storms in West Cornwall history blew up. The walls of Penzance promenade were breached in several places, flying slates brought peril to those walking in the streets, trees were blown down, and buildings near the sea were flooded. There was no abatement next morning, and Jane's Carbineer remained in the Orlyt which was heaving in the gale and swaying, and I swore would at any second crash into smithereens. Hence I warned Jane not to open the door to collect her daffodils.

The morning passed and the violence continued. She had entered the Carbineer for the Prince of Wales's Cup at the Penzance Flower Snow, the elite daffodil cup of the show, and they had to be in place at the Show by that evening. They had to be specially arranged, and the cup of each daffodil had to be open in such a way that the professional judges would approve.

'Don't,' I said to Jane, as in the late afternoon I set off to drive to the station with our daffodil boxes, 'don't open the door while I'm away.' Then I added, looking at Jeannie: 'It's now your responsibility to see that she doesn't.'

When I returned, the terrible storm was still at its height . . . and the Carbineer had been removed from their corner in the Orlyt. They were indoors, and Jane was arranging them, and smiling, and Jeannie was smiling too.

Next day Jane won the cup of the daffodil elite, the youngest competitor ever to do so.

There were sentimental reasons, therefore, for me to maintain the Orlyt and, whether Geoffrey left or stayed, this would have to be done. As for the other four greenhouses, each seventy feet long, these too were not in good condition; and I visioned myself on my own collecting the broken glass when the gales blew, and fixing new panes, and I didn't care for the prospect.

Our main crop, however, was daffodils, but they were not nearly so demanding as tomatoes. If we had been truly professional we should have dug them every two or three years, split up the bulbs, sterilised them and transplanted them but, apart from the time and expense involved, we had not enough land to do this. Much of our twenty acres is steep, rocky land, and the meadows too small for the use of bulb lifting and bulb planting machines. Hence, for the most part, our bulbs stayed in the ground for year after year, although each year Geoffrey had been able to dig up and transplant a ton or so. Inevitably disease would cull some of the bulbs, but we had to risk that;

and, in any case, we were comforted by the sight of the daffodils which bloomed year after year in the hedgerows and, in particular, by a variety called Cromwell, which had been planted in the stable meadow fifty years before, and still bloomed profusely every spring.

As for the rush of daffodil harvest time, the problem of coping with it was not as difficult as it might seem. The extent of the rush depended, of course, on the weather and, for this reason, we hated mild springs. For the past four years without fail there had been mild springs, and this had resulted in a telescoped season with every Cornish grower trying to pick the daffodils before the buds burst. Once upon a time the market only wanted fully out blooms, but now the situation has been absurdly reversed and the market dislikes even half-open buds. Thus every year we pray for a cold spring, no sun, clouds every day, in order that the daffodils mature gently and so ease the labour problems. Nevertheless, even if the season was a rush, I believed we could manage it. We had helpers to draw upon and, in any case, Jeannie and I rejoiced in getting up at dawn and working hard to dusk during daffodil time whatever the weather.

Indeed this was the mood which enveloped us as we continued to discuss what we should do. Commercial reasons apart, we wanted to be free again, to wake up in the morning and to be beholden to no one.

'Jeannie,' I said, 'I know what we will do.'

'Tell me.'

'Let's be patient for a month and see what happens to the tomatoes. If it is a bonanza of a season, we will go on as at present. If it is a flop . . . well . . .'

'All right,' said Jeannie.

And I guessed which alternative she would prefer.

FOUR

The tomatoes held their price for a fortnight, then began to dip. I, however, continued to dither. I preferred to wake up in the morning and place a metaphorical blanket over my mind, and go out to talk to Geoffrey as if everything was normal. It was a classic example of indecisiveness on my part, the passive wait for an event to force my hand. As for Geoffrey, he too was acting. He may not have been aware that Jeannie and I were wanting to be on our own again, but he was aware that his wages were beyond what any small business such as ours could pay. Thus he too was waiting for a decision as he went about his daily work.

It was on Monday of the fourth week that the decision at last was made. I began the day normally enough by playing my role of Martha. Martha was the name A. P. Herbert used to call Jeannie, after the biblical Martha, the servant, who was always so busy looking after other people; and then later, when I was seduced into helping with the housework, Jeannie would sometimes call *me* Martha. 'The windows need cleaning, Martha,' she might say. Or she might declare: 'The frames of the pictures need dusting, Martha.'

There are, of course, gentlemen Marthas everywhere today. It is a growth industry, and very rightly so. Some of us are more conscientious than others, willing to take on tasks which a few years ago we would not have dreamt of bothering about. I cannot say that I am the ideal Martha, not even a conscientious one, but I do have spasmodic moments of activity which meet with Jeannie's approval.

On this occasion I was vacuum cleaning the carpet in the sitting room, and the long cord became entangled in my legs, then in the legs of a chair.

'Damn the thing,' I said. No blame on the vacuum cleaner. All because I was clumsy.

Jeannie was in the tiny bedroom, changing sheets. I am sure officialdom would disapprove of our bedroom, so small is it; and I am certain there would be a howl of protest from council house tenants if they were provided with a bedroom of its size. We are happy with it. We have a lovely view lying in bed looking through the window down the lane and across the valley. Oliver and Ambrose like it, jumping in and out of the window from a little stone edifice beneath the window, built there specially by me to make the jump easy . . . then often making me regret my kind gesture because they take charge of large sections of the bed, and my knees ache, and Jeannie groans that she is being squashed.

Pleasant though it is, we have many times discussed imaginary plans of having another bedroom, adding one to the cottage that would be more appropriate to modern living. Our cottage consists of our tiny bedroom, the living room, the porch, the spare room which was originally designed as a chicken house, and a pint sized bathroom. All wonderfully convenient and satisfying, but it doesn't prevent us from sometimes wishing we were a pools winner, or the surprise inheritors of a large sum of money, so that we could, with discrimination, add to the cottage. We rent Minack and, although all the improvements we have made have been at our own expense, we will never be able to own Minack. Our landlord and his family have possessed farms in the area for generations, and cherish them as the 'Western farms' ... he is enlightened, leaves us on our own, but we still dream of a day when we might go to him and say: 'Will you sell Minack?'

I steered the vacuum cleaner under my kidney shaped Regency desk, then round by the record player and the untidy pile of records which lay underneath it. It is a catholic collection of records. It is a collection to suit moods rather than to cater for a knowledge of music. Karajan conducting the Berlin Philharmonic in Die Walküre and Götterdämmerung, numerous Chopin records, Richard Burton reciting Dylan Thomas, Gertrude Lawrence and Noël Coward in the balcony scene of Private Lives, Previn conducting the London Symphony Orchestra in Rachmaninoff's Second Symphony, Previn when he was a dance band pianist, early Beatle records, Herb Alpert, Fauré's Requiem (which I first heard when it was chosen by Margot Fonteyn on Desert Island Discs), the piano works of Brahms and Debussy, Ravel's Daphnis and Chloe, and many others which, after long intervals, I suddenly have the urge to play.

Then there are the records of Chamber Music. For much of my life I had ignored Chamber Music, believing it had no message for me, preferring instead the majesty and excitement of great orchestras playing the music of the masters ('What music do you like best?' someone asked Sibelius; 'Sibelius,' Sibelius replied, 'always Sibelius.') One day a couple called Don and Joan Edwards and their son David, who was at Clifton and who was soon to win a scholarship to Oxford, brought two Amadeus records for us, Haydn and Mozart String Quartets. We had never met the three of them before. They arrived at the door of the cottage explaining they liked my books and that they wanted to give us something in return. That 'something' has opened our minds to the pleasure of Chamber Music, for which we will be forever grateful; and we now have a library of Haydn and Mozart, of

Beethoven and Brahms, of Fauré, Borodin, Dvorak and Rossini.

My record player is a good one, but I am continually tantalised by the advertisements extolling the special virtues of this record player or that pair of loudspeakers, this turntable or that amplifier. I meet an expert on such matters like David Edwards and I become even more confused. He kindly wrote to me a nine page exposition of all the alternatives open to me, and left me bewildered despite the fact that his letter was written with such clarity and skill that I found it a delight to read. The point is that Hi-Fi sound is like a musical rainbow. The perfection, it seems, can never be caught, and thus the Hi-Fi addicts become so involved in the technicalities, too much bass here, too much treble there, that they are unable to sit back and simply enjoy the music.

My friend David, however, combines his Hi-Fi expertise with a profound love of music, and his Hi-Fi letter to me was in essence an example of the art of correspondence, an art which has been all but destroyed by the rush of modern living, television, and the telephone. I have from time to time other correspondence with him, and recently I asked him if he could find for me the quotation of Joseph Conrad's definition of literature; and without delay came the answer that it came from the preface of Conrad's *The Nigger of the Narcissus*.

'My task,' Conrad wrote, 'which I am trying to achieve is, by the power of the written word to make you hear, to make you feel . . . it is before all to make you see. That . . . and no more, and it is everything.'

David went on in his letter to discuss Shelley.

'To play the quotations game,' he wrote, 'how about this from Shelley, the most important neglected writer of today . . . he's talking specifically of poetry, but I think you can feel your work is a response to exactly the same need . . .

' "We want," said Shelley, "the creative faculty to

imagine that which we know; we want the generous impulse to act that which we imagine; we want the poetry of life; our calculations have outworn our conceptions; we have eaten more than we can digest. The cultivation of those sciences which have enlarged the limits of the empire of man over the external world has for want of the poetical faculty proportionally circumscribed those of the internal world; and man, having enslaved the elements, remains himself a slave." '

And there was Malcolm Sutton who acted in much the same way, erudite letters and thoughtfulness. He came walking down the winding lane at the age of nineteen, soon after I had written *A Gull on the Roof*, and told us that he came from Chester, where he was studying to be an organist. He failed in his final examination at the Royal College of Music due, as he put it, to terrible nervousness on the day and, though he could not now be a professional musician, he had become one in mind; and he has composed many pieces, and has had particular success with his setting to choral music of Roger Venable's poem *Combe Valley*, Roger Venables, author of that Oxford classic *Portrait of a Don*. Malcolm has been coming to Lamorna every year since he first came to Minack, and he is accepted by everyone as belonging to the valley; and his work is often performed by Sampson Hosking and his Lamorna Choir. He too has given us records . . . Delius's *Song of the Hills* and, when I mentioned that I had heard Charles Widor's *Toccata* at A. P. Herbert's memorial service at St Martin's in the Fields, a week or so later he sent us a record of it played by the organist of Chester Cathedral.

I pushed the vacuum cleaner back into the centre of the room to clean the rugs. We have three rugs covering the carpet, and they madden us. They shift, curl in humps, all on their own. I will flatten one, or all three of them, so that they are flush with the carpet; and then I will go out, we both will go out, for a walk or to do our work, and when we return the rugs are certain to have a ridge in each of them. The rugs are alive. Nobody has been present to move them. Jeannie alleges that Hobberdy Dick is responsible.

Hobberdy Dick, as explained by his creator K. M. Briggs, is an imp who inhabits old houses, looks after the inhabitants in mysterious ways provided he approves of them, guards them against evil, and is occasionally mischievous. His particular mischief is to hide things. Thus, if something is lost, Jeannie, who is an admirer of Hobberdy, will say that Hobberdy has hidden it, and say this in a tone of voice which suggests she is sure that in due course Hobberdy will return it.

For instance, she attributes to Hobberdy the mystery of the missing pair of Georgian silver salad servers which had been given to us as a wedding present. Some time ago they disappeared. Jeannie searched for them in every corner of the cottage, and eventually resigned herself into believing they had been stolen . . . or perhaps, as she tried to persuade me, that Hobberdy had taken them and would in due course return them. A few weeks ago these beautiful and valuable silver salad servers reappeared. Where? Lying on a rock outside the door with the silver untarnished. No human being had visited us that morning. So was there substance in Jeannie's belief in Hobberdy?

Recently Hobberdy played another trick on Jeannie, or, more accurately, for a while he was blamed for the incident.

Two friends of ours, Ken and Arunda Peters, were coming to lunch, both of whom, Jeannie as a good hostess remembered, had a special liking for after lunch coffee of a particular coffee bean. Ken Peters was a top newspaper executive in Aberdeen, and the first time we met them both they were standing by the stone wall alongside the barn, Ken wearing a Cameronian kilt. They were wanting to come up to the cottage and introduce themselves, but were hesitant to do so. Since that day, they have been many times to Minack, and their friendship has been one of our enriching experiences.

For breakfast, on the day of the lunch, Jeannie ground a few of the coffee beans, which are described as Pure Mocha and Mysore, for ourselves . . . but, just as she had completed the grinding, the plastic top of the electric grinder flew off. Jeannie did not immediately look for it. She wanted her breakfast.

I went out for an hour or so after breakfast and, when I returned, bringing with me a freshly cut lettuce, a cucumber, freshly picked tomatoes, all to accompany the crab which came from Newlyn fish market, I was greeted by cries from Jeannie, the cries of a hostess in a panic.

'I can't find the plastic top! I've searched everywhere! All these special coffee beans, and I won't be able to grind them!'

'Calm, Jeannie, calm,' I soothed. 'It must be there somewhere in the kitchen.'

'It isn't! I've had everything out. All the pots and pans. Not a sign!'

The kitchen, being very small, hardly room for two people to stand in, didn't offer many places for a plastic top to hide.

'Maybe it fell behind the stove,' I said. 'Or behind the fridge. Let me have a look.'

I peered this way and that.

'No, it's not there . . . but I've an idea. What about the dustbin, or the compost heap? I saw you take things out to throw away.'

'Yes, I did that.'

'All right. I'll go and have a look.'

For the next half hour I sifted the dustbin, distastefully taking everything out, and I prodded the compost heap, and raked it with a trowel. Memories of past meals, but no plastic top.

'There is only one thing I can do,' I said, when I

55

returned to Jeannie. 'I'll have to go into Penzance and buy a new grinder.'

'Oh, you can't do that!'

'Yes, I will . . . you *must* be able to give the Peters their coffee beans.'

It was at this moment that Hobberdy had pity upon us. For there was a sudden cry from Jeannie: 'I've found it!'

Hanging in the kitchen is a row of kitchen knives, kitchen spoons, and a special scoop of a spoon. Flush inside the scoop was the plastic top.

Hobberdy's most remarkable antic, however, has only just occurred.

For the past two days Jeannie has been searching for the special cat comb she uses for Oliver and Ambrose. It is a comb she has had for a couple of years, replacing another comb she lost, a comb which had a three inch handle. She looked everywhere during the past two days, and finally decided this morning that she would have to buy yet a third comb.

The post duly arrived, and one of the items was a small parcel. She opened it . . . and there was the comb. Not the one she had just lost, but the comb with the handle that she had lost two years ago!

The parcel had come from a summer visitor who had bought one of Jeannie's drawings and to whom Jeannie had posted the drawing.

Jeannie is a very careful packer, and obviously a drawing in its glass frame has to be very carefully packed. Yet somehow, without Jeannie having a clue how it happened, the long lost comb was packed too.

How did Hobberdy manage it?

I completed my carpet cleaning and Jeannie her bed-making, and then I went outside to see how Geoffrey was progressing with the tomato picking. He had finished, and was now grading and weighing them. About forty twelve-pound chips he expected to have, and I told him to give me a shout when he had finished, and that I would take them in myself to the wholesalers in Penzance.

An hour later I arrived at their premises on the harbour front, backing the Volvo into their covered yard to make it easy to unload, and hailed Harold, the foreman, with the news: 'I've got forty for you!'

'Too bad,' he said. 'Too bad.'

'Why's that?'

'The price is on the floor . . . we're flooded with tomatoes. Still trying to sell those you brought in on Friday.'

'What price are you asking for them then?'

'70p.'

'70p!' I shouted.

'We'll be lucky to get that.'

'But that's the sort of price we got ten years ago when wages were £15 a week!'

'It's bad, it's bad . . . but it can't be helped.'

'How do you explain it? It's still July. There are holidaymakers everywhere. Expect it to drop in August when the coldhouse lot come in, but not now!'

'That's the way it is.'

Having indulged in my outburst, I helped unload the chips from the car, carrying them into the store and stacking them alongside the many others that were already there; and as I did so I found myself being suffused by a delightful calmness. This is it, I said to myself. This is the event that I have been waiting for.

'Harold,' I said, as I got back in the car, 'it's a great day.'

He looked at me puzzled. He had always done his best for us. It was not his fault the price was on the floor.

'Why?' he asked.

'One day I will explain,' I replied, as the car began to move.

I did not waste any time when I returned to the cottage. I hastened to find Jeannie, and gave her the news, excitedly, as if we had won a victory; and so we had in a way.

'The price is on the floor! And not a chance that it will improve!'

'Don't be *too* happy,' she said.

'I'm only relieved. That's why I'm excited. We are out of the doldrums.'

'When will you tell Geoffrey?'

'I'm going to face up to it straightaway.'

'Don't immediately. Let's work out what you are going to say.'

The end of an era. An upheaval. A routine busted. The moment of dismissal is always frightening, whatever the reasons. And yet when an hour later I told Geoffrey he showed no surprise. He too was relieved that the waiting was over.

'You'll get the redundancy money,' I said, 'around £500.'

'As much as that?'

There was a gleam in his eye.

'And you can stay on for three months, of which three weeks will be your holiday period . . . of course, if you want to leave for another job beforehand that's OK with us.'

That afternoon at 5 pm as he buzzed up the lane on his motorcycle, he seemed to be a happy man. And he remained willing and happy for the rest of his time with us . . . at the end of which, he immediately had the job of a grocery salesman driving a motorised shop, a job of which he has made a great success.

I had, in the meanwhile, been keeping a watch on the swallows nesting on the ledge beneath the attic in the barn. I had erected an elaborate anti-cat defence of wire netting which would block any cat's attempt to reach it; and I was not just thinking of Oliver and Ambrose as potential culprits. There were the roaming farm cats as well, which from time to time meandered our way. I had also divided the barn into two by fixing a wooden windbreak down the middle, thus providing the shelter for Penny and

Fred in one half, and safety for the swallows from donkey noses in the other half. The space for Penny and Fred was cramped, but I decided they had to put up with it. After what had happened to the first nest, I was taking every precaution from such a disaster being repeated. My activity might have upset the swallows, but they continued to fly in and out of the barn, to chase each other in the sky, and to twitter on the apex of the roof; and of course, as soon as I had completed the defences, I left them on their own.

Swallows, it has always seemed to me, are by nature happy birds, while robins are wistful, chaffinches bossy, dunnocks busy, and blue tits perky. I remember at my preparatory school a master telling my class to make such a descriptive list of what we thought of the birds in the countryside, an enlightening thing to do because it brought home to me, young as I was, that the birds around us were part of the universe and not just flying objects to take for granted, or to be shot.

Shooting, in my youth, was part of my family environment, and my father, despite being a kind man, had great pleasure in taking part in organised shoots. I too, because I belonged to a world of conventional, unthinking standards, took part in organised shoots; and I used to stay, for instance, with a young friend at a large Norfolk estate where the highlight of a September day would be to lie in wait at dusk behind a hedge, gun cocked, and to listen for the singing flight of duck coming home to roost; and to shoot them as they glided down to the reeds. Bang! Bang! I was being true to my conventional upbringing. I had ignored the lesson my schoolmaster had tried to teach me.

Yet to do myself justice, and my father, I did not shoot for the sake of killing. I shot for the pot. I was a hunter. My father had always made it clear that it was a crime to shoot without reason. Sadly there are many fathers today who do not hold this view. They give their sons airguns for which, incredibly, no licence is required; and the sons proceed to shoot at any moving thing.

At the end of July, with the help of a mirror that I held up to reflect the inside of the nest, I found three eggs, and they lay among a bed of downy gull feathers. Now came the period when I had to act as a bodyguard. Geoffrey was warned not to go into the barn under any circumstances and, when a visitor arrived and parked his car outside the barn, I quickly ushered him away from the vicinity. Nothing was to be allowed to disturb the swallows this time. All was going to be well.

The summer days passed by, and the swallows played joyously in the sky; and when at intervals the lady was sitting on the eggs, the gentleman would often be on the roof of the barn twittering away by himself, as if he were telling the world he was the luckiest of swallows to have a safe nest below him with three eggs that were soon to be hatched.

I knew the day when they were hatched by the sudden activity which surrounded the barn. No idle twitter on the roof. Instead there was a frantic rush in and out of the barn, diving through the doorway minute after minute, diving sometimes between Fred's ears as he stood in the opening, sweeping the sky for insects. A couple from Cape Province in South Africa called on us at this time.

'They set off from our district,' the man said, 'a month before we flew to England. Funny to meet swallows again so soon.'

'Funny,' but the records are clear. Time and again swallows ringed in Britain have been found during our winter months in South Africa. A bird ringed in Scotland at Stirling was recovered in the Transvaal; another ringed at Aberdeen in July was recovered in Cape Province in December the same year, and another ringed in Essex was also recovered in Cape Province, four months later. Swallow journeys have for me the same magic as astronauts landing on the moon, without the expense.

One morning, along with my mirror, I slipped into the barn, held up the mirror, and saw the three nestlings, beaks open, believing food was being brought to them; and I marvelled that within a few weeks these tiny things would have the strength and the instinct to set off on a journey of six thousand miles. From the Minack barn to Spain, across the Straits of Gibraltar to Morocco, down the West Coast of Africa, Ivory Coast, Ghana, Nigeria, Congo, Angola, and then reaching their journey's end, only to return within a few months. Such an achievement places human conceit in perspective. Our belief in reason, our worship of passing fashions, our endless desire to search for mirages as substitutes for true happiness, disappear into irrelevancy when one realises the majesty of a swallow's travels.

'They'll be flying any time now,' I said to Jeannie one night ten days later. I was lying in bed, window wide open, framing the stars.

'We'll have to keep a special watch on Oliver and Ambrose when they start fluttering around the barn,' answered Jeannie.

'They don't flutter for long,' I said. 'They learn to fly very quickly.'

An owl hooted in the wood, and a minute later it hooted again, loudly, as if it were close to the cottage, perhaps on the wall behind the white seat. In Monty's time there was an owl which used to perch there hooting at Monty on the gravel below like a yapping dog.

'Is Ambrose in?' I murmured, putting my hand out and touching Oliver in the middle of the bed.

'Don't know.'

Silence for a moment, then an urgent hiccuping hoot, the hoot of an owl who was highly excited.

'I bet he's seen Ambrose.'

'Perhaps,' said Jeannie sleepily.

The following morning I had another look at the nest. I waited until I saw both the swallows come out of the

61

barn, and fly into the sky above the stable meadow, and disappear across the valley. I darted into the barn, mirror in my hand, and saw again the three little swallows jostling together. Still another few days, I guessed, before their first flight.

That afternoon the weather began to change. The wind shifted to the south, grew stronger until soon a gale was beating against the leaves of the elm trees; and with the gale the rain came, and scudding low clouds blotted the view of Mount's Bay from our sight. By nightfall a winter storm in summer was blowing around the cottage.

We went to bed early, the wind rattling the half-open window. Oliver and Ambrose curled up on the sofa, and both of us ready for sleep. Suddenly I heard above the storm the hoot of the owl. Then several hoots in rapid succession.

'That damn owl,' I said, 'gets over-excited.'

It was an unpleasant sound, cruel, so different from the usual, quiet hoot.

'Anyhow we know it's not Ambrose he's after.'

It was noon the next day that I began to notice the silence around the barn. The storm had calmed down and, though the wind was still blowing strongly from the south, and heavy showers were frequent, there was no viciousness in the weather. Why the absence of the swallows flying in and out of the barn? The weather was not bad enough to stop them chasing the insects. The young had to be fed, and frequently fed. So why the stillness? Why no sight of the swallows?

In late afternoon the wind edged round to the west, and the skies cleared, and the air became full of soft scents, damp earth, tobacco plants, roses; and the sky above the barn was still empty of swallows. I became uneasy. I had to find out what had happened.

I didn't tell Jeannie what I was about to do. I didn't tell her what I was fearing. I didn't want her to share my apprehension, for she was inclined to be too emotional in such a situation.

Thus I went alone with my mirror to look at the nest on the ledge beneath the wooden planks of the attic; and I found it empty.

Had the three flown away? I could not believe that this could have been so. They were still fledglings. What about the condition of the nest? The downy feathers of the gulls had been ruffled, but the nest had not been vandalised. It was still intact. Surely if a cat, despite my defences, had attacked it, there would have been a clawing at the mud edges, and these would have crumbled. What *could* have happened?

After I told Jeannie, the two of us went round and round the subject, and we could find no answer. We were sure that Oliver and Ambrose in any case were innocent. They had spent the night indoors. Nor was there any sign that a roaming farm cat could have reached the nest. So what had taken the three nestlings which I had taken such care to protect?

The macabre explanation, and the macabre coincidence came next day.

We have a hut in the wood where we store potatoes and fruit, and each of us has used it from time to time to write in.

That afternoon I went there to collect some potatoes, and when I reached the door and started to turn the handle, I suddenly saw what lay at my feet.

The three little swallow nestlings lay there. They had been regurgitated.

The owl had taken them.

FIVE

'Goodbye, Geoffrey,' I said, 'except it isn't goodbye, we'll see you in the village.'

The first Friday in October, Geoffrey with red helmet, wheeling his motorbike out of the shelter.

'We'll have a pasty,' he said.

An old joke. Whenever I had said I was going to the pub for a drink, or if on a morning I said I had had too good a night out, Geoffrey would make his joke. 'Going to have a pasty?' Or: 'Too many pasties last night?' I cannot remember how this joke was started. Some time long ago when he first came to Minack.

He got astride his bike as Jeannie came down the path.

'Goodbye, Geoffrey, good luck,' she said.

I wondered how he felt. After all he knew every corner of Minack, had worked every piece of ground in all seasons, and so in a way Minack was part of him. Yet there seemed to be no sadness in this moment of departure. We were being formal in our goodbyes, formal at this end of an era. All of us were glad that the waiting was over.

He thumped the starter with his foot, once, twice, and the engine sparked, and ticked over for a minute as we all said goodbye again; and then he was away, across Monty's Leap and up the winding lane, leaving us to listen to the fading noise of the machine, a noise we had heard a thousand times, up the hill, until he passed the farm buildings at the top, and there was silence.

'We're alone, Jeannie,' I said, taking her arm. 'How wonderful!'

'Did you give him anything extra?'

'Above his redundancy?'

'Yes.'

'I did . . . something we didn't really want.'

'What was that?'

'The Merrytiller.'

She took her arm away from me.

'But that's worth at least £100 these days.'

'Well,' I said, 'it was in poor condition, and we haven't used it for a long time . . .'

'But you *might* have wanted to use it again . . . and anyhow I remember I bought it, after Mummy died. Was he grateful?'

'You know, in Geoffrey fashion.'

'I do think you might have asked me first.'

'I'm sorry, I ask forgiveness.'

'I understand, though I still wish you had asked me.'

We had reached the cottage door.

'Anyhow,' I said, 'all this is over now. We are free. We're never going to start the day listening to the motor-bike arriving, and me wondering what to ask him to do. No wages to pay out on Friday, no PAYE forms to fill in, no bewildering orders from the Agricultural Wages Board to try to interpret. Do you know what I had from them this morning? It was a blessing really that they chose this day to send it to me. It just underlines one part of the bliss of being on one's own. Just listen to this.'

I went over to my desk and picked up a printed piece of paper containing the following language:

Where in any week (whether the worker is employed by one employer by the week, or by any period longer than a week), total payment at the minimum rate of wages, that is to say the minimum weekly rate for the standard number of hours together with payment in respect of overtime and eligible night work, made under the provisions of paragraphs 1, 4 and 5 of this part of the Schedule to a whole time worker shown in column (a) of the table below exceeds the corresponding amount shown in column (b), the minimum rate payable to any such worker shall be the said total payment, reduced by the amount shown in column (c), to which shall be added 5 per cent or the sum shown in column (d) whichever is the lesser amount, by way of an earnings supplement.

'That, Jeannie,' I said, 'is the sort of thing I'm going to be spared.'

'It's incomprehensible!'

'To me it is too.'

It is the disease of the age, language like that. Society is so involved in the business of maintaining freedom that it tangles itself in verbal chains, losing thereby the very freedom it sets out to preserve. Freedom, in the old meaning of the word, depended upon a give and take, a moral sense of what was right or wrong, for its preservation. Today, however, our civilisation has become so complicated, our values so warped, political pressure on government so great, that freedom has become an illusion for ordinary people. Freedom is now only a word repeated parrot fashion by our leaders as they rush from making one new law to making another. Freedom has become a mountain of regulations that few can understand.

It was an Indian Summer of an October evening, and I said to Jeannie that I would fetch drinks for the two of us, and take them up to the bridge; and when we arrived there Oliver came around the corner of the *escallonia* a moment later. I was always touched by his endearing habit of appearing from nowhere when we sat down on the bridge. He might be settled in the greenhouse, or on the garage roof, or among the grass beneath the apple tree, or in any of his other hideouts . . . but some telepathy always told him when we were on the bridge, and he would appear. Ambrose also would sometimes appear, a little nervously, watching us, watching Oliver as he turned upside down as cats do when they are requesting a tickle, and one felt that Ambrose was wondering why Oliver should behave in such a manner. For he was one cat who never requested such attention. He might sometimes turn upside down, but he would do so at a distance. He did not want a tickle. If you approached him to do so, he would leap to his feet and hurry away. A tickle was undignified.

We sat there looking across to the other side of the shallow valley where the black steers of our friend Bill Trevorrow quietly munched the grass, and over in the far corner on the right, the far corner where we first saw Oliver, Oliver who on that occasion pounced on a mouse and missed, were a pair of magpies coarsely chattering on the ground. Suddenly a fox appeared near one of them, and glided down the field close to the hedge, and the magpies followed, hopping as if they were feathered kangaroos, and hurling rude epithets at the fox as they did so. Why are magpies so rude to foxes? I have seen them time and again following a fox, either on the ground, or by flying from bush to bush harshly cackling at him when he is hidden from view in the undergrowth; and I have never seen a fox answer the insults by making a show of attacking the magpies. As usual, the fox disdainfully ignored them on this occasion, then jumped the hedge and disappeared into a thicket of blackthorn which led to the cliff.

'Strange, isn't it,' I said, 'how full of contradictions we are.'

'I don't think contradictions are unusual in people,' Jeannie replied. 'Everyone has them in one way or another. Only the computer wants to make people Mr and Mrs Average.'

'Some people have more contradictions than others then,' I said. 'Take you, for instance. You write sophisticated novels, and write for *Gourmet*, the most elegant magazine in America, and when you go to London the management of the Savoy, or the Berkeley, or Claridges, are always ready to give you a suite larger in size than the cottage, and everyone makes a fuss of you.'

'Naturally I enjoy it. It's an echo of the past.'

'That's one of the contradictions. You enjoy the luxury life, and yet you are perfectly content to live a peasant-like life here at Minack.'

'Not really a contradiction, because I never want that kind of life for more than a few days.'

I am amused by Jeannie when she goes to London, not that a visit happens very often. She slips into the role she used to lead as if time had not intervened. Hotel porters greet her, head waiters welcome her, and flowers fill her suite; and she behaves with a quiet assurance which suggests she is a permanent fixture in this world of sophistication.

When Jeannie's novel *Home is the Hotel* was published, Susie Orde, the Press Officer of the Savoy Group, gave a luncheon party in Jeannie's honour in the Savoy Restaurant . . . Susie, who is the contemporary Jeannie in the Savoy world. The guests gathered in the American bar, where we drank champagne; and then we walked down the steps to the hall, turning left down the further steps to the restaurant. It was now, as we walked to the round table in the centre of the restaurant, that an incident took place, displaying the style of Jeannie, that I will always remember.

She caught sight of the figure of Trompetto, the famous master chef of the restaurant, at the far side of the room standing at the entrance to the kitchens; and Jeannie, intuitively experienced in such matters, knew that this meant he had paid her the compliment of preparing the lunch personally himself . . . and she immediately left the rest of us and walked over to thank him. It was a memorable menu: *Le Jambon de Parme et Poire Courice*, *Les Truite Saumones Royale* (salmon trout poached in champagne with a delicate cream sauce), *Le Sorbet à la Menthe*, and *Cigarettes au Chocolat*. Later that day, she was paid another compliment. We were guests at Claridges for dinner (Jeannie had written an article about Claridges for *Gourmet*), and when we sat down Jeannie admired the arrangement of flowers on the table. At the end of the evening François, the maître d'hôtel, gave her both the flowers and the bowl in which they were arranged; and these were so carefully packed that when we returned to Minack next day the arrangement was still intact.

High above us as we sat there on the bridge was the white plume of an air liner coming in from the Atlantic and heading east to Heathrow. I took from my pocket a tiny transistor with an airband wavelength, pulled out the aerial, and pointed it skywards. A few seconds later came the sound of the air liner's captain announcing that he was passing Land's End, that he had three hundred and five passengers aboard including fifteen children, and that there was a stretcher case aboard, and that he also required a wheelchair on arrival.

I put the transistor back in my pocket.

'One of *my* contradictions,' I laughed. 'All my talk of the joys of the simple life, and yet I delight in gadgets like a transistor which picks up aircraft flying over Minack.'

Jeannie had bought it for me at a time when three nights a week around nine o'clock a sonic boom burst over West Cornwall . . . Concorde had arrived from Washington. At first it was officially denied that it was Concorde, but we already knew the denial was inaccurate. A retired doctor friend had monitored Concorde on his own set, and this inspired Jeannie to buy an airband set for me. It is a fascinating, tantalising toy; tantalising because aircraft captains often talk in code numbers, meaningless to me. However, I now have maps of the aircraft routes which pass over Land's End; and so I can look up into the sky and speak knowledgeably to a companion. I point to a plume and tell him the air liner is on the way to Cork, or to the Azores, or to the Caribbean, or coming from Washington or Kennedy; and sometimes, when I am pointing, the aerial of the transistor pointing too, I score a

70

coup. A voice sounds clearly on the transistor: 'This is Concorde. Can I have Oceanic Clearance?'

I am, therefore, a gadget man although, to be fair to myself, I am normally a practical gadget man. If armed with the correct gadgets, all of us have an extra day in the week compared with people of thirty years or so ago. Dish washers, washing machines, food mixers, coffee percolators, the efficiency of gas and electric stoves, washing powders, powerful carpet cleaners, machine type do-it-yourself implements, and so on . . . all these help to give us the extra day. Then there are the outdoor implements. Instead of slowly digging the garden, there is the rotovator. Instead of pushing the lawn mower, there is the engine-driven mower. Instead of clipping the hedge, there is an electric hedgecutter. All these implements contribute to the extra day.

'Then there is the contradiction in our attitude to people,' I went on. 'We treasure privacy, hate crowds, could never tolerate community living, prefer the loneliness of a winter to the busy times of summer, and yet when we meet people, most people at any rate, we are genuinely interested in them, and are stimulated by them.'

'Only the givers,' said Jeannie, 'not the takers.'

'That's only fair to ourselves. We have to riddle out those who take up our time in order to fill their own time.'

'How many have you riddled out?'

There was a teasing note in Jeannie's voice.

'One must be careful of course,' I replied. 'One doesn't want to avoid people who are genuinely interested, or vulnerable people, shy people, or people who have come a long way . . .

'But how many *have* you put through the riddle?'

'I started riddling this week.'

Jeannie laughed.

'Who were the victims?'

'Nobody in particular. I was riddling out those in my

71

mind who drag one down, melt one's enthusiasm. People with narrow horizons.'

'And people who are nosey,' added Jeannie.

Sometimes one can laugh at the nosey ones. In two successive weeks of the daffodil season we were visited by ladies who were at school with Jeannie, and whom Jeannie had not seen since. The first one arrived in a torrent of rain just at the moment we were carrying in the baskets of Joseph Macleod. Jeannie was wrapped in oilskins in defence from the storm; and the old school friend whom Jeannie couldn't remember greeted her with astonishment:

'*What* are you doing? You *can't* be gardening in this weather!'

The second lady, the following week, also looked at Jeannie with astonishment, Jeannie who was working hard to despatch as many daffodils as she could pack for the afternoon train . . .

'Don't let me interrupt you,' said the lady as she dallied beside us. 'I have a garden too, so I know *what* work is involved.'

She had half an acre.

Of course there are those who are puzzled by us. They cannot in their minds pigeon-hole us, and to pigeon-hole everyone, place them in neat categories, is what many people, including the media, like to do.

'Quite extraordinary,' said one media lady to Jeannie, looking around the tiny kitchen, 'the way you write *such* sophisticated novels, when you have to admit that you can't possibly say where you live *is* sophisticated.'

The truth is that neither of us has the patience to cultivate showmanship. We are uncomfortable when asked to promote ourselves. We do not wish to seek out applause. Our wish is to enjoy the life we have chosen, to share it with others, and to survive. But outward appearances are important among many people. Occupy a house which impresses the visitor, be always in the forefront of

72

the Keep Up With The Jones's Brigade, and their egos are satisfied.

Jeannie and I, however, have never had any inclination to join the Keep Up With The Jones's Brigade. We are, for instance, neither party goers nor party givers, though we both delight in prolonged conversation with a small circle of companions. Parties fragment my mind. Party talk, with its trail of inconclusive sentences, leaves me in a vacuum, and I lose the rhythm of my life, taking a day or two to return to it. I have inquests as to what I have said, or not said, and a vague dissatisfaction pervades me. I find it difficult to concentrate on my task whether it be writing, or attending to correspondence, or weeding a row of carrots. I am, for the time being, insensitive to small pleasures, the small pleasures which provide the base for happiness in the country. This attitude, no doubt, is a weakness on my part. I ought to be able to divide my life into compartments, cope with social occasions, and then revert to my normal life without ado. But it is not so. Hence I can rightly be labelled an insecure person, that derogatory phrase so often used by psychiatrists. I am, however, glad to be such a person. I would far rather be full of self-doubts than someone who is always sure of himself.

The chastity belt between us and a social life is that we have, by choice, no telephone. We are spared, therefore, the person who on a whim might ask us out. The lack of one also has other uses. If some event, or some action of anyone upsets us, we have time to contemplate before responding to it.

The Queens, the hotel on the promenade at Penzance, was from where for years we used to telephone. It was then a family owned hotel, run impeccably on old fashioned standards. It had long service staff, and our particular friends were Frank Williams the barman, and Billy Tunmore the head porter. Both had been at the hotel since they were boys, and Frank had retired shortly before a take-over took place. Billy had still a year to go before retiring after fifty years on the staff when the sale was completed, and for some reason the new management did not believe he would be suitable for the new style of running the hotel. One week we saw his usual cheerful self in the front hall, the next week, when we went in, he had gone.

Hotel head porters, as Jeannie in her hotel expert capacity always insists, are key members of a hotel staff. They give the visitor his first welcome, give him information about the surrounding area, what to do and what to see, and generally take care of his day to day arrangements. A friendly, efficient head porter is, therefore, a considerable asset to a hotel; and Billy was certainly friendly and efficient and was known as such by visitors from all over the world. He was also in charge of the switchboard, and he would dial our numbers for us, and tell us that the call was through, and direct us into the appropriate telephone box; and afterwards we would pay him. It was an ideal arrangement for us. No dropping coins in a slot. We could telephone where we liked, and as long as we liked, as if in the privacy of our own home. Hardly, however, a profitable addition to the Queens Hotel income . . . although, as a result, we recommended many people to stay there, and I wrote about Frank and Billy; and Billy was once persuaded to be on a BBC TV programme with us. But when the new management took over and Billy left, the switchboard was removed, a coin telephone kiosk installed instead, and several other innovations were introduced. The new management was right to do so. Clients of the old fashioned Queens were a dying breed. The new income groups, both home and foreign, had to be catered for. The Queens is now an admirable hotel of its kind. A new kind. A bulk tourist kind.

So now we go to the kiosk at Sheffield where the cottages lie either side of the road to Penzance, a village of which no one can explain how it obtained such a Yorkshire name; and we also sometimes go to the kiosk at

Sparnon which stands at the corner of the Porthcurno via St Buryan–Penzance road, and the Porthcurno via Sheffield–Penzance road. All these country kiosks are looked after by local ladies, who are paid 25p a week to keep them clean and to take care of anything that by mistake was left in them. In the case of the Sparnon kiosk, the lady in charge took such pride in her work that she achieved national notoriety, including a photograph and article in the *Sunday Times*, and of course the inevitable television.

It was as if she fell in love with her kiosk. She placed a carpet on the floor, had a notebook and pencil for the benefit of the telephone users, kept a vase of fresh flowers on the small ledge and, at Christmas, helped by her children, decorated the kiosk with holly and silver ribbon. The kiosk became a tourist attraction. People would come to it and ring up far off friends just to say that they were telephoning from the most cared for kiosk in the country. Once we had a critical conversation in this kiosk about a cat called Felix who had been left behind at a farm after the owner had sold it. I told this story in *Cottage on a Cliff*, and at the end of the chapter is a drawing of the kiosk drawn by Jeannie. No one cares for the kiosk now; Mrs Richards, the lady in charge, had to leave Sparnon to live in Penzance.

The light was fading, it was growing chilly on the bridge.
'I'm going in now,' said Jeannie.
'I'll fetch the donkeys.'
'Want any help?'
'I can manage.'
The donkeys were in the field above the cottage, but I always took them down to the field in front of the barn at night. It meant that they could shelter in the barn if the weather became rough; and as dusk fell they usually were waiting for me to take them down, standing side by side by the small wrought iron gate. I would open the gate, put on their halters, and lead them down the steep gravel

path, sometimes with difficulty because Fred would go one way and Penny the other, or both would try to have their fill of *escallonia* leaves in the hedge beside the bridge, and I would tug them away, calling them to stop, and then suddenly obeying me, they would choose to rush down the path, forcing me to behave as if I had lost control. It was usually a minor adventure, putting the donkeys to bed at night.

I went up to the gate on this occasion, picked up the halters from where they were lying in the grass, and found Fred waiting for me, but no Penny.

'Where's your mum?' I said and, by addressing a donkey in such a way, I was behaving quite normally. I see nothing to be ashamed about in talking to an animal.

Fred did not move, and I scanned the field and caught sight of Penny on the far side, standing by the hedge close to the wood.

'Stay here, Fred,' I said, 'while I fetch her.'

I walked across the field and, as I neared her, Penny began to move towards me, and I made some endearing remarks, put on the halter, and walked back across the field, Penny being perfectly happy to come with me. I put the other halter on Fred, and proceeded to lead them both through the small gate, and on the few yards to the steep gravel path. To reach this path, which passes between the escallonia and the uneven stones that is the approach to the cottage door, you have to pass through a narrow gap between two stone hedges; and every now and again during the past week or two, Penny when she had reached this gap, had come to a full stop, and had refused to budge.

'Come on, Penny,' I would call, tugging at the halter. 'Come on!'

After a couple of times of her displaying this obstinate, though curious, behaviour, I said to Jeannie that I had a whimsical explanation. I said she had stopped because she had seen Lama's ghost. Her stopping place was a favourite spot of Lama's.

On this occasion she stopped again, put her head down as if she were looking at something close to the ground, and anchored her feet. Fred, meanwhile, my left arm outstretched, holding his halter, was devouring the *escallonia*.

'Come *on*, Penny!'

I had them both safely down in due course, watched them meander off into the centre of the field, and returned to Jeannie.

'Have any trouble?'

She was poaching a lemon sole, bought from Newlyn that morning.

'Penny a bit slow . . . and she saw Lama's ghost again.'

'Do you think Penny is well?'

'Why do you say that?'

'Obvious . . . after all, it was you who got the vet.'

I had asked the vet to have a look at Penny a couple of times during the late summer because she had seemed lackadaisical. A visitor would arrive and ask to see the donkeys and, while Fred would scamper over to see what was up, Penny, I had noticed, would linger behind.

'The vet said he could see nothing wrong about her, and after all he's known her since she came here.'

'Forget it . . . it was just that the thought went through my mind.'

'I'll tell you what we'll do,' I said. 'If it's fine tomorrow, we'll take them on the donkey walk.'

The donkey walk runs along the cliff to Carn Barges, and then inland towards Lamorna.

'Before breakfast?'

'Yes.'

'Good idea.'

SIX

The morning was fine, visibility across Mount's Bay was good . . . and the fog-horn was sounding.

'Blast that thing,' I said.

The fog-horn came from the Tater-du automatic lighthouse which is over the hill from us, less than a mile away. It is controlled from Penzance on the advice of coastguards at the Lizard, thirty miles away, or at Gwennap Head five miles away; and whenever they have fog in their area they inform the Penzance Trinity House depot, and the duty officer presses a button, and the Tater-du fog-horn goes into action, whether or not there is fog on our particular coast.

'The donkeys will have to wait,' I said to Jeannie.

'It's so clear,' she replied, 'they must switch it off soon.'

A fog-horn in thick fog is a mysterious, even a romantic sound, and when Tater-du blares in such conditions it is also a comforting sound. Wayward yachtsmen are being warned, sleepy foreign sailors are woken up, and we are spared the prospect of a wreck on our coast and the consequent horde of ghoulish sightseers.

It is when the weather is clear, when there is no justifiable reason for the fog-horn, that the sound of it grates. Sometimes, when the sound has persisted despite the fact that we can see ships on the horizon, I have

79

despairingly driven to the telephone kiosk at Sheffield, and called the Penzance depot, and a conciliatory duty officer has tried to soothe my irritation.

'It's the Lizard . . . they told me to switch it on.'

'Well, ask them to tell you to switch it off.'

My request is sometimes granted, and I return to peace and silence at Minack, and the congratulations of Jeannie.

The noise of the fog-horn varies in its intensity. We are cushioned by the hill from the worst of it and, sometimes, we do not hear it at all. For a fog-horn is, in fact, an unreliable warning system. A fog-horn depends upon the direction of the wind for its effectiveness. Thus, if the wind is in a northerly direction, it blows the sound out to sea but, if it is a southerly, the sound is blown inland and, as a result, especially if it is a gale, boats a mile off shore scarcely hear it.

But we hear it on the donkey walk, the cliff path to Carn Barges and the path inland towards Lamorna. It blasts into our ears and on a fine day when the visibility is clear, the sea quietly rippling the rocks below, it vexes us. Hence we do not take the donkeys on a walk. Hence, as on this occasion, we wait until the noise has stopped.

I put the halter on Fred, and began leading him to the gate which opened onto the big field overlooking the sea, known as Fred's field because it was beside a rock in this field that he was born. Penny waited behind. She always waited until Jeannie joined her. She had a special affinity with Jeannie, as any animal is inclined to have with one special member of a family. Penny did not have a halter. It was not necessary for her to have one, although we carried it with us in case of emergency, in case Penny was in one of her ebullient moods. Normally she was quiet and docile, but then occasionally there was this mood when she appeared to say to Fred: 'Let's escape from *them*. Let's run away on our own!' And if we were not on the alert, she would suddenly barge past us on the narrow path and Fred, who, once through the big field, was also let off the halter, would follow her at speed. Many a time the donkey walk has ended with Jeannie and me out of breath after catching up with the donkeys now quietly grazing at some far off patch of grass, and no doubt amused at our distress.

I keep Fred on the halter as we walk through the big field because, otherwise, he might dash off in some other direction and, instead of a walk, we would be chasing him round the meadows. I hold him by the halter, therefore, until we reach the three feet high hedge which divides our land from the Carn Barges side. It is a hedge in the form of a stile. It is flat at the top, easy for walkers to climb over. Easy too, from the Minack side, for donkeys. They jump on the top, and jump down the other side, and the walk proper begins. It is different, however, on the return because the jump is a little higher, and it has to be made at an angle, and although it is a simple jump, the donkeys have sometimes had inhibitions about it; Fred in particular. Fred would go too close to the hedge, like a showjumper who is refusing a fence, then back away, then go too close again, and we would urge him to be sensible and to give himself plenty of room for the jump; and, in the end, it was usually Penny who solved the hold-up by pushing past Fred, and showing him how easily the jump could be done.

I was first over the hedge this time, followed by Fred and a leisurely Penny, and Jeannie. I walked at a normal pace towards Carn Barges, brushing the brambles and blackthorn closing in on the path, Fred sometimes nudging me in the back, past the dying bracken, up and down the boulders that lie like giant stepping stones on the path, until Jeannie called out from behind me: 'Penny's stopped. She won't move.'

I turned round, meeting Fred head on.

'She's seen another ghost,' I said, jokingly.

There was a trace of anxiety in Jeannie's voice, just a trace, as if she was allowing her imagination to see trouble, although in reality it was not there. All Penny had done was to stop, just because she had a wish to stop, and she was soon to be stepping forward again.

Yet there was a reason for Jeannie's reaction. Penny had developed a habit of picking up her right hind leg as she walked. She lifted it from the ground, and gave it a kind of flick, before setting it down again. It seemed to us that the habit was particularly pronounced when the ground was wet; and so, because we were naive in such matters, we explained it away for a long time by saying she was behaving like a dandy, a Regency dandy who hated the touch of mud. Then one day, when the vet had paid us a call, we mentioned it to him, and he explained that it was not dandyism on her part, that it was in fact a nervous twitch called *string-halt*.

'No cure,' he said, 'and no harm in it.'

Nor did it cause any pain. It was just a twitch, like a human being can have a twitch.

But there were other factors which caused that trace of anxiety on Jeannie's part. Three years before Penny had been struck by laminitis. This is a very painful inflammation of the sole of the foot, and it usually occurs in spring when a donkey eats too much growing grass. It is a form of indigestion and, once a donkey has experienced it, it is likely to recur each year; and sometimes the pain and discomfort is so serious that the donkey has to be put down. The symptoms are severe lameness, an unwillingness to move, and the hoof feels very hot to the touch. The cure, the momentary cure, is an injection of cortisone, frequent bathing of the hoof with cold water, and a determined effort to keep the donkey (or pony, or horse, for that matter) moving. If she remains stationary, she eventually may collapse.

This is what had happened to Penny; and if it had not been for Fred, she might not have survived. Fred, who had known no other donkey except his mother, had a devotion to her which was sometimes even hurtful to watch. He would never go out of sight of her and if, by any chance, we led Penny out of a field, leaving him behind, he would bellow his distress and race round the field in a vain attempt to find a gap in the hedge which would enable him to dash through and re-join her.

It was an early May morning, six o'clock, when I was woken up by the hysterical hee-haws of Fred; and when I dashed out to see what was the cause of it, I found him in the paddock heaving himself against the wood fence, as if he were trying to push it down and get out. There was no sign of Penny, no sign of her in any part of the field, until suddenly I caught sight of two black ears showing just above the grass at the far end. She was in a terrible state when I reached her, eyes glazed, and her head swaying, then flopping her head down with a bump onto the ground, where she lay quite still except for her heavy breathing.

Jeannie stayed with her while I hastened away to telephone the vet, a sleepy vet, who made no complaint at being disturbed, and who was standing beside Penny within the hour. Penny was her old self a week later, and she had never suffered again from laminitis. But it was Fred, trumpeting the alarm, who had saved her.

There was another event, however, a recent one; only a month before in fact which had sent me again into a panic. Jeannie had gone into Penzance on her weekly visit, and I had been into the field where the donkeys were grazing, for the sole purpose to have a talk with them. I make this sort of visit quite often, not so much to amuse the donkeys as to amuse myself. I feel in need of a diversion, and so I go to the donkeys; and the donkeys, as often as not, will turn their bottoms to me, and continue their grazing. Then, in order to gain their interest, I endeavour to make them play; and an easy way to do this is to take a box of matches from my pocket, run up behind Fred, and rattle it. This sends him off away from me in a spurt; and, to keep the pressure up, I run after him, continuing to rattle the matchbox. Often I have played the same trick with Penny; and so an observer, if he happened to be in the neighbourhood at the appropriate time, could have seen me running round the field, two donkeys racing ahead of a box of matches which I violently rattled as soon as I was within noise-rattle distance of their tails.

My moment of panic was the day when I went to the field to play my game and found Penny lying flat on the ground. I urged her to get up with encouraging words. Not a movement. Then suddenly she stirred, slowly gathered her feet under her, and heaved herself into a standing position, and began to inch forwards . . . inch is the word. It almost seemed her hind legs were paralysed.

'Come on, Penny,' I said, putting my arm around her neck. 'Let's go a walk across the field.'

She inched forwards, then came to a full stop. I was scared.

Off I went to telephone but, because Jeannie had the car, I had to ask permission to telephone the vet from one of my neighbours; and although my neighbours are kind and sympathetic, I do not like doing so. I did not want them to share my distress. I did not want to make any illness of Penny a subject of general conversation.

A while later, three vets arrived, not one. The three of them had been engaged on an operation on a cow in the neighbourhood, and their office had told them about Penny, and they came as soon as the operation was completed.

In the meantime, Penny's situation had changed. It had changed dramatically. No sooner had I returned from telephoning the vet than I saw her walking around the field quite normally. I grew anxious, not because of Penny, but of causing the vet unnecessary trouble when he was so busy. I even wished to see Penny contrive a limp, any gesture I hoped she would make in order to prove that I wasn't just a hysterical, hypochondriac donkey owner.

She had no intention of helping me. She proceeded to graze unconcernedly around the field, not a trace of discomfort; and the three vets, after examining her closely, pronounced her perfectly fit. But why had she behaved as she had done?

We reached Carn Barges on our walk, and we paused, the donkeys silhouetted against the sea, munching the grass around the great Carn. It is a curious Carn, curious in that details of it appear in no guide book and I can find no historical reference to it, and when I asked an old parson called Crofts, who wrote the history of St Buryan parish, he was unable to offer any explanation of how it was placed there.

It is of course overshadowed by the legend of the Logan Rock four miles along the coast. Two legends, in fact. First the legend of how this giant rock was so balanced on a supporting rock that a push could set it in motion; and the second legend of the young naval lieutenant who set out to defy an ancient Cornish prophecy that no human power would ever succeed in overturning the Logan Rock.

In 1824 the lieutenant proved this prophecy false, and with unfortunate consequences to himself. He organised crew members of the cutter he commanded to place several levers under the Rock and, when they were in position, he gave the order: 'Heave!' . . . and over the cliff the Rock rolled. Miraculously, it lodged in a crevice, instead of crashing into the sea below; and this resulted in the lieutenant receiving his punishment.

The vandalism had been witnessed by two local men, who reported it to the local authorities, who reported it to the Admiralty; and there was soon such a brou-ha-ha about the event that the Admiralty decided to take vigorous action. The lieutenant was ordered to return the Rock to its original position . . . and at his own expense.

The dilemma of the lieutenant had a subconscious effect on me during my childhood, for, on the walls of one of the rooms of my Cornish home, hung engravings which depicted the efforts of the lieutenant to restore the Rock to its original position. The pictures scared me, gave me a warning of the retribution that comes to those who commit foolish deeds without thought of the consequences. There were graphic pictures of the beams which were planted about the fallen Rock, and the chains which were passed round it, and the pulleys which were rigged, and the capstans being manned. After a week's hard labour, the Rock was retrieved, though it was never restored to its former perfection of balance. As for the lieutenant, he spent the rest of his life paying for the cost of the restoration . . . and just before his death, he paid the last remaining debt, and paid it with interest.

A mile away from the Logan Rock is the Minack Theatre, carved out of the cliff in a majestic setting overlooking the sea. Here, on summer evenings when the weather is fine, splendid theatrical productions are staged; and anyone who visits the theatre, sitting on the stone seats, the night sky the ceiling, the moon streaming on the waves below, finds it a memorable experience.

The Minack of Minack Theatre is pronounced Minnack. Our own Minack is pronounced Mynack. Our map name is Dorminack, but it has been known locally as Mynack ever since anyone can remember; and when I began writing the Minack Chronicles, I chose to use the shortened name.

At the time, the theatre was little known and was referred to as the Open Air Theatre (it is named as such on the current Ordnance Survey map), and direction signs to this effect were at local cross roads. After I had written three books of the Minack Chronicles, the Open Air Theatre signs were dropped, and Minack Theatre signs substituted; and this, unfortunately, resulted in some confusion between the two Minacks.

The then manager of the theatre wrote to me about this confusion, suggesting that I should use Dorminack instead of Minack and that, if I did so, he promised to remove all the pins stuck in the Tangye effigy on his mantelpiece. I replied by proposing a meeting, but the meeting never took place.

Carn Barges, like the Logan, is also balanced on a supporting rock, though it is far too solid ever to be pushed into motion like the Logan. Barges is the Cornish for buzzard or kite and so presumably it received its name because of the habit of buzzards to perch on the top of it. It is a massive piece of granite, and it is so placed on the supporting rock that it looks like a giant statue standing on a plinth. The question is, how was it placed there? The Logan Rock was a natural phenomenon, and Carn Barges probably is too. But it is also possible that man, aeons ago, may have manoeuvred it there. Yet how could he have done it? And for what reason? A sailor's guide, possibly, for standing as it does high above sea level, it can be seen for miles out to sea. Yet *how* did man manoeuvre it there, *if* he did?

The Carn has significance for Jeannie and me because when standing beside it after walking along the track from Lamorna Cove, we first saw the grey stone cottage of Minack; and had this powerful intuitive feeling that it held our future. There we were, Jeannie on a brief holiday from the Savoy Hotel; and we saw this grey spot across the moorland and nestling beside a wood, and we *knew* it was to become our home. Heavens, the difficulties that lay ahead to prove this true were enormous, but when at last it was achieved, when at last we had shaken off the shackles of our comfortable though exciting life in London, we experienced this exquisite feeling of relief. No waking up in the early hours and being appalled at the prospect of the programme that filled the day ahead, no mental inquests, real or imaginary, of what went wrong the day before, no fears of plots among envious colleagues, no noise, no time-keeping, no stress artificially created by one's own imagination. The Carn, standing there, part of our landscape as we move around Minack, is the emblem of the freedom that we relish.

It means other things too. Monty of *A Cat in the Window* once walked with us on a May morning through the bluebells to the Carn, taking time off during the walk to investigate badger holes and to sniff the trace of a rabbit or of a fox; and when he reached the Carn, he jumped on the rock which I call a plinth, and settled himself there for a rest. He lay there, like a miniature Trafalgar Square lion, purring, the sea calling far below him, swallows coming in from the south, a stonechat bouncing his tail in excitement a few yards below him, bird calls everywhere . . . I remember that moment, and remember another a few years later which occurred at exactly the same spot where Monty lay.

I was gazing out from the cottage towards the Carn one day when I saw a strange activity taking place around it. In that particular period, before the advent of the Coastal Path, it was rare to see anyone on the Carn. Indeed, when A. P. Herbert, wit, politician, author of musical plays, used to stay with us and he saw anyone on the Carn, he would cry out in the manner of American Indians of long ago: 'White men! White men!'

This particular strange activity that I saw involved three young men from a tropical continent, who were wielding a large and heavy sledge-hammer on the plinth upon which Carn Barges was balanced. A vandalism repeat, in fact, though in a different form, of what had happened to the Logan Rock.

Within twenty minutes, however, I had raced across the moorland and was able to stop them doing any further damage; and they explained that all they were trying to do was to take samples of the granite for scientific examination. Nevertheless, for the rest of time, the splintered granite, the ragged edge of the plinth where Monty had lain and purred, will be a memorial to their visit to this country.

As for the buzzard aspect of Carn Barges, I have never seen a buzzard perch on the top of the Carn. Buzzards often hover above the moor and, soaring effortlessly in the currents of the air, call to each other with cries that sound like the mewing of a cat in the sky; and this spring a pair began building a nest in a cleft of the cliff nearby to Carn Barges.

I could still see the clumsy spread of sticks as I stood there beside the donkeys, and I was sad that the pair never stayed to have their young. When they started to build, it was early April, and strangers in the area were rare; and no doubt the pair believed they had chosen a desolate spot of the Cornish cliffs where they could be undisturbed through the nesting period. Unfortunately, they did not know what could happen in the Lamorna area on Good Fridays. In the olden days a tradition was created about Lamorna on Good Fridays . . . a tradition in which boys and girls who were courting would spend the day there, and they came from all parts of Cornwall. It was a harmless, pastoral occasion and, in the evening, there was dancing on the quay. Today, however, police patrol Lamorna on Good Fridays, the cafe is closed, the inhabitants are on guard, and motorbikes from distant parts roar up and down the road. Some people then roam further afield, transistors blaring, shouting to each other on the rocks. After this Good Friday I never saw our pair of buzzards again.

We turned inland after we left Carn Barges along the path which leads to the lane above the valley of Lamorna; and it is a path which would never have been there had it not been for ourselves and Jenny Napper. Jenny, at one time, organised a subscription among those who wanted to use such a path, for the cost of a local man to cut it open; and, once done, Jeannie and I and the donkeys continued the good work, the donkeys consuming tasty brambles as they passed while I, with secateurs or a slasher, cut down, or did my best to cut down, the invading undergrowth. The path led to a stream and at the point where the donkeys jumped across was a water pump which,

before there were mains, provided the water for the five houses on the top of Lamorna valley; and it was Fred Napper with the gnarled arthritic hands who used to look after this pump.

On this occasion we did not go beyond the stream. The donkeys were idling, giving the impression they did not want the normal long donkey walk which would have taken them across the stream, up the path several hundred yards, until just short of the lane above Lamorna valley we turned right, and took the path which led to what we call the far feeding grounds. A beautiful plateau, reached by passing through an archway, knee high and prickly, of gorse. Scores of times we have done this walk with Fred and Penny, but on this morning, this early October morning, it was clear that the donkeys had had enough when they had reached the stream.

Therefore, we turned back and, as Frankie Howerd might say, a funny thing happened on the way home. A couple suddenly appeared, strangers as far as we were concerned to the area, from the direction of Carn Barges, to which we were returning.

The sight of two donkeys suddenly encountered on a lonely path, you might think, would excite curiosity. But neither made any remark at all. They pressed on past us. Caricatures of English folk in contact with strangers.

They were the witnesses too of an event, had they but known it, which for ever will sadden our lives. This was the last occasion that Penny was ever to reach that stream; and we might have sensed this when, on coming back from the walk, we reached the wall over which Fred was so often hesitant to jump, waiting for Penny to be the leader . . . for, on this occasion, it was Penny who refused to jump, and it was Fred who was the leader.

SEVEN

A week later we set out on the donkey walk again. Penny seemed happy enough when we started off but, as soon as we reached the stile at the bottom of Fred's field, she refused to budge. Fred jumped over it, but Penny anchored her feet.

We again had no special cause for concern, for in every other aspect she was appearing to be normal enough, although of course she had her twitch, and I had noticed that the twitch was now accompanied by a click.

However, having accepted the fact she had no wish to jump the stile, we returned to the cottage . . . and then, on reaching the barn, Penny made a roguish gesture of turning right up the lane, trotting happily up to Monty's Leap and over it, and trotting so fast that I called to Jeannie to hold Fred while I raced after her with a halter. I caught her, and she was clearly disappointed at being caught; and so, in view of this ebullience on her part, I proposed that we should take the two of them on a walk up the lane. The walk, also, could have a purpose. I had a message I wanted to leave for a friend who was to stay at the Menwinnion Hotel; and it was a pleasant walk, up the hill and past the farm buildings at the top, then along the lane, until turning right, just at the point of meeting the main road.

93

There was nothing amiss with Penny on this walk and we went up the lane, past the gate through which Jeannie once rode Penny, Lama in her arms, and me leading a very young Fred . . . and Penny suddenly took off, and threw Jeannie and, while Lama ran off unhurt, Jeannie lay in the lane, semi-conscious. Jeannie's fault, as she admitted. She had behaved, in riding Penny with Lama in her arms, with over-confidence. She didn't blame Penny.

We went on up the hill past Jack and Alice Cockram's farmhouse. Jack was a London evacuee of World War II, but he stayed on after the war to become a farm labourer and married a local girl whose father, a carpenter, Abner Grenfell, fashioned the window frames of the cottage; and whose uncle, Jim Grenfell, kept the St Buryan pub for many years. Then past the Trevorrow farmhouse. The Trevorrow's, Bill and Kath, now live in a bungalow further down the lane, while younger members of their family live in the farmhouse; and, on passing the farmhouse, we saw Walter's van with Walter sitting in it, and his plethora of cats around him, some on the bonnet, some on the roof, some in a circle around the van.

Walter, I call a pied piper of cats. He has been a partner of Jack Cockram for many years, but he does not live at the farm. He lives in St Buryan, belongs to one of the most ancient families in the area, is a bachelor, suffers from blindness in one eye after a chipping struck it when one day many years ago he was repairing the lane; and ever since I first met him he has teased me about Jeannie.

'Oh, I envy you, I do,' he says to me, looking at Jeannie, 'you lucky man.'

'Plenty of girls after you, Walter.'

'Not likely.'

He has a beautiful collection of cats. They roam about the farm buildings, raise families in the hay, wander in safety around the fields, and assemble in contented anticipation beside the van at meal times.

'Fred's looking fine,' he said, as we passed.

'Penny's looking good too, don't you think?' I said.

He paused.

'Getting on, isn't she?'

'Only seventeen.'

'Oh, there's plenty of time in her yet. Over in St Just I knew a donkey who had turned forty.'

I put my arm round Penny.

'Hear that, Penny?'

We left Walter and went on up the lane and, as we reached the Trevorrow bungalow, Bill appeared at the gate.

'Like a swede?'

'Lovely.'

'Here you are then.'

And he handed us a couple, trimmed of their roots, trimmed of their foliage.

'Early, aren't they?' said Jeannie, thanking him.

'A little, perhaps. But there'll be plenty more. Just ask when you want them.'

There is this pleasant camaraderie in our neighbourhood; a naturalness in the wish to be content, and, therefore, the best in others is looked for, not the worst; and there is this barter . . . swedes for daffodils, tomatoes for milk, while at the appropriate season there is also broccoli, offered to us when we pass the big barn at the end of the lane where Owen Prowse and his father, Enoch, pack their broccoli into crates.

'Go on, have one,' urges Owen.

'But you're getting a terrific price!'

'Oh, go on, have one!'

Owen, just out of school, helped us to dig potatoes one season; and while he shovelled up the row, turning each plant to one side which Jeannie, as the picker up, would shake, then put the good size potatoes in one basket, the small ones in another . . . as he shovelled and she picked up, he used to tell her of his ambitions.

He was going to be a famous racing motorcyclist, he was going to race on the Isle of Man, he was going to devote his life to motorcycles. It hasn't worked out that way, though he is happy enough with his sweet wife and young family in the farm that he runs, just off the lane and not far off where it joins the main road.

His father, Enoch, and his mother, Linda, we have known since we first came to Minack. They live in a neat farmhouse, half-way up Boleigh Hill, which is very popular with those seeking bed and breakfast; and I often see Enoch trudging up the hill on the way to help Owen on his farm. Enoch is cadaverous looking, spare, and with long white hair which makes him look like the biblical character of his name. He was at the end of the lane when we reached it, standing by the milk stand opposite the big barn where the broccoli is packed. We had to turn right with the donkeys, not on the main road, but on the narrow road which led to Menwinnion . . . but, for no good reason that I could see, the donkeys suddenly went on strike. They would go no further. We pulled and pulled on their halters, but they were adamant. They would *not* go to Menwinnion.

At this moment, Enoch walked across to us . . .

'I'll get them to move,' he said, grinning.

And there followed such a torrent of unbiblical language that the donkeys were startled into activity.

'There you are,' he said, 'easy.'

Easy it was. The donkeys walked quietly for the rest of the way; and just as quietly on their return.

Penny enjoyed the walk. There is no doubt about that. When she came back approaching Monty's Leap, she was trotting happily along, and Fred was dutifully following her. Nor did she show any signs the next day, or the next few days, of being lame or, for that matter, of behaving in a desultory manner. Indeed she had recovered her best form; and I forgot about her refusal to jump the stile, and the nagging feeling that I had that she was not well.

96

But a week later, I suggested to Jeannie that we might take the donkeys to the onion meadow, where they could spend the morning; and so we set off to take them there before we had our breakfast.

The onion meadow, traditionally so named because, presumably once upon a time, onions were grown there, borders the land we once rented for the growing of early potatoes, a period in which we visioned ourselves becoming the largest growers of early potatoes in our area. The onion meadow itself, however, has a shallow soil, only rough grass grows there, but it is grass which has always been favoured by the donkeys.

I started off with Fred, expecting Jeannie to follow me with Penny, who was in the small yard in front of the barn, but she called out that Penny did not seem to wish to go. I still expected her to follow, and I was continuing on my way with Fred when Fred, suddenly realising that Penny was not behind him, turned round and went galloping back, hooting at the same time. He raced round into the yard, nearly knocking Jeannie over, and stopped beside Penny as if he were asking her: 'Are you all right?'

It so happened that this time we believed we had a clear explanation for her behaviour. We had been waiting for the past few days for Kenny the farrier to come to pare the donkeys' feet, for it was obvious that Penny's hooves had become too long for comfort. We had had this trouble with Penny ever since she first came to Minack. Her feet had been badly neglected in the past and, once this neglect has reached a certain stage, a donkey's foot can never again be in perfect condition. Thus it was with Penny. Her feet were so mis-shapen when she came to us that all Kenny our farrier could do was to control them from becoming even worse. Fred, on the other hand, looked after by Kenny from the beginning, had feet that a prize donkey would be proud of.

Kenny arrived the following morning, and it was a nervous moment for me. Geoffrey had always been in charge of the donkeys during Kenny's previous visits, and I was apprehensive as to whether I would have the strength to hold them while Kenny performed his task. Sometimes Fred, sometimes Penny, sometimes both of them, would behave like bucking broncoes; and Geoffrey would struggle to hold on to the halter while they reared up on their hind legs, Kenny beneath them. A terrifying sight; and now it was up to me to put myself in Geoffrey's place.

I had, however, formulated a plan. Jeannie, at my suggestion, had bought a packet of chocolate biscuits; and so, when Kenny, the tools for paring ready, waited for me to lead Penny to him, Jeannie came too, chocolate biscuits in hand, ready to thrust the biscuits at either of the donkeys who might threaten a bad-tempered outburst. The ruse was successful. First Penny, then Fred, and they caused no trouble at all. Soothing words and chocolate biscuits made them as amenable as could be.

'Good as angels,' said Kenny, when he had finished.

The angels went off into the field and began munching grass, and I was relieved to see Penny walking normally. Perhaps she *had* been waiting for her feet to be pared, and that was the real reason why she had refused to jump the stile, why she had refused to join Fred on the walk to the onion meadow. It was comforting to think so; and, on the face of it, it seemed sensible.

That night, for a few minutes, I thought my optimism was confirmed, irritatingly at that.

Around one in the morning, I was awoken by the sound of hooves on the chipping stones outside our bedroom window.

'The donkeys are out!' I shouted, semi-consciously, and causing Jeannie to jump out of her sleep, crying: 'What? What? Where? Where?'

It is a menacing sound, hooves on chipping stones, when you are half asleep. One conjures up the donkeys galloping up the lane, on, on, on, and finding themselves on the main road, and continuing to gallop, to the left or to the right, towards Land's End or towards Penzance, with early morning cars dashing towards them.

Therefore I jumped out of bed, seized the torch, put on a dressing gown, and hurried outside. Had I left a gate open? Surely not. And anyhow, where were the donkeys when I went to bed last night? Half asleep, I couldn't for the moment remember; and then I realised that I had left them in the field above the cottage, and had not taken them down to the stable field beside the barn; and so with the torch I walked delicately up to the gate, delicately because I hadn't been able to find my slippers, and I was in bare feet. I reached the small iron gate which leads to the field, found it closed, then shone the torch round the field until the light caught the two donkeys. Penny and Fred had their bottoms to me. They were staring, ears erect, like spaniels pointing, through the bare branches of the trees down towards the barn.

I left the gate, and began to walk down the path to the stable meadow, then decided, because I now knew the donkeys were safe, to put on my slippers and, for that matter, to put on a thick jersey for, although it was warm for a late November night, there was a strong breeze blowing from the west. I went into the cottage and found Jeannie waiting for me, already dressed.

'What's going on?'

'Heaven knows. The donkeys are all right.'

'Perhaps it's the steers again.'

'Must be . . . can't think what else.'

'I'm ready to come with you.'

We had been invaded twice in recent weeks by a concourse of steers, twenty or thirty of them, from the farm to the west of us. Fortunately, they had never reached the immediate neighbourhood of the cottage, but they had careered over our meadows, tearing off branches of the hedges, and trampling all over the bulb ground. No real damage was done, because no bulbs were growing.

But we were wrong about the steers.

When we arrived down at the barn and shone the light onto the field, there standing in the middle were two horses.

'Where on earth have they come from?' I said.

We shut them in and, next morning, we set out to solve the mystery. It took us a couple of hours to do so, ringing the police, calling in at the blacksmith, and asking anyone who might help us; and eventually we found the answer.

They had escaped from a field three miles away towards Land's End, had careered along the main road, ignoring any turns to the left or to the right, until they came to the Minack lane; and down the lane they galloped to wake us up and give us a fright and to provide a delightful diversion for the donkeys. Fred was sorry when the owner arrived to take them away. 'Hee-haw, hee-haw!' he called after them.

The weather changed into rain and gales a week later, and it continued like this until the third week in December; and then suddenly there was a day when the rain clouds fled away, and it was soft and warm, as if it were a day of early summer. So, instead of the donkeys standing out there in the wet looking lugubrious, their bottoms to a hedge, and refusing obstinately to take shelter in the barn which was there awaiting them, they were able to doze in the sunshine. But we were still apprehensive about Penny because she continued to move slowly compared with the briskness of Fred; and as the Christmas holiday was coming, we thought it wise for the vet to look her over again.

A couple of days before the vet came, however, Penny, as if she were wanting to demonstrate that there was nothing for us to worry about and that we were victims of our own imagination, suddenly gave Jeannie a hilarious time.

I was in Penzance, when Jeannie decided to take the donkeys up from the stable meadow to the field above the cottage; and though she put a halter on Fred, she didn't put one on Penny. She led Fred up to the field, took off the halter when Fred had got through the gate but, instead of finding Penny obediently behind her, suddenly she saw Penny dashing up the path to the well and the clothes line. She said afterwards that it was such a joyous sight to see Penny behaving with such abandon that she forgot she had not shut the gate; and so, when she went after Penny, Fred was quick to take advantage; and Jeannie found herself coping with two donkeys who were experiencing their idea of bliss . . . that of running free where they shouldn't be running at all, and who were now determined to make the most of it.

Thus they raced for a minute or two up and down to the clothes line, then into the field which we call Lama's field that is adjacent to where the clothes line is hoisted, and round and round it, kicking up their heels in delight, and with Penny always in front, leading Fred.

Then, having tired of this field, having laughed their heads off in having Jeannie chasing them, Penny proceeded to jump down three stone steps by the spot we call the bridge, and to rush down the path, and left past the rose garden, and into the orchard, Fred dutifully in pursuit.

Eventually, of course, the donkeys tired of the game, and allowed Jeannie to catch them; and then meekly allowed her to take them back to the field above the cottage where, not making the mistake again, she firmly took care to shut the gate.

When I returned, she told me the story with laughter and happiness. For, after all, she said, no donkey who had a chronic ailment could have behaved with such gay abandon.

Nevertheless, when the vet came on the 22nd, she *was* lame, or she behaved as if she were lame; and we were glad he had arrived. I was still half-thinking that Penny was pretending, because I could not believe that a lame donkey could have behaved in such a way as Jeannie had described. But the vet took the matter seriously. The sheer excitement of that occasion, he suggested, may have made her ignore any pain she might have had; and so he recommended that we should bathe her hooves with cold water, as it would seem that she had been attacked again by laminitis.

What was puzzling, however, was that laminitis usually came with the lush grass of spring, and the symptom was a very hot hoof. Penny's hooves, on the contrary, were cool to touch. Nor did she show any signs of pain when we touched them; and, indeed, when I deliberately squeezed them with my fingers, she gave no special reaction whatsoever. She appeared to be normal . . . and yet there was this lameness.

On December 23rd, after bathing her hooves according to the vet's instructions, we went into Penzance to collect our Christmas supplies; and we decided that, on the way home, we would call in on Jenny Napper and wish her a happy Christmas. It was a yearly ritual to call in at Christmas time, and Jeannie always took her a small present. Jenny Napper appreciated elegance, style, or however you might like to describe articles of true quality; and this time Jeannie had bought for her from Jenners in Edinburgh a sachet of pot-pourri edged with real lace. Jeannie wrapped it in soft yellow paper, tucking in on top a white camellia, picked from our camellia bush at the side of the rose garden.

Jenny greeted us with her usual warmth and, although we only stayed ten minutes, we had our customary happy time with her. She was suffering, however, from the results of a bad fall a fortnight before and, when Jeannie asked her whether she had seen a doctor, she said she hadn't bothered to do so. Jeannie pressed her to change her mind and, aware of the feyness in Jenny, she brought Fred Napper into the scene. Fred, said Jeannie, *wanted* her to see a doctor, adding that she felt Fred's presence in the room at that moment, almost a physical presence, and that he was urging that the doctor should be called for. Jeannie said to me afterwards that she was not inventing this emotion, and that she really did feel Fred was there. Anyhow her efforts seemed to succeed, and Jenny promised to contact the doctor.

She came to the door to say goodbye to us, wishing all at Minack a happy Christmas, and with a special message of love for Penny and Fred.

I was active on Christmas Eve, rotovating the ground of two of the greenhouses, and clearing the small greenhouse in readiness for the bunching of daffodils, which was likely to begin in the middle of January. The small greenhouse is a dump for most of the year for all sorts of things I don't know what to do with. The benches are covered with old newspapers and cardboard boxes, and garden tools which I don't use, but which I might use. Periodically I enthusiastically clear it all up, and this Christmas Eve was one of those occasions.

But for Jeannie and me Christmas Eve was pivoted on the ceremony of the mince pies, the ceremony which had taken place every year since Penny first came to Minack, and Fred was born. At quarter to twelve we always lit a candle in the old barn, and as the light flickered on the rough whitewashed walls, we gave the donkeys Jeannie's specially made mince pies. It was a short ceremony, only ten minutes, because we always left before the clock struck twelve. Donkeys, according to a tradition, kneel at that moment . . . and we wanted to keep the illusion of that tradition intact.

On this occasion the donkeys came into the barn just as I was trying to light the candle which stands in an old fashioned candle holder on the ledge of the right hand window. They had followed Jeannie in, noses up in the air, sniffing the mince pies which Jeannie had on a plate, tempting them by holding the plate just above their heads.

I struck a match, held it against the wick, and had no response. I had not touched the candle since the previous

Christmas Eve, for part of the ceremony was that the candle was always the same candle, though becoming lower each year; and I once said to Jeannie that when the time came for a new candle, we would be entering a new era of our life at Minack.

I struck the match again and held it against the wick. Then again. I came to the conclusion that dampness must be the cause of the failure, and a shiver went through me. Why this of all years should the candle not light? And then on the fourth attempt there was a sudden flare . . . not a simple candle flame, but as if I had lit petrol. It flared for a second or two, then as suddenly died down; and I saw that in a mysterious way the candle had completely melted and, although it was now alight, the flame came from a collapsed candle, a sort of plateau of a candle.

The light flickered, however, around the old barn, and I saw two happy donkey faces being teased by Jeannie . . . a mince pie just held out of reach. Maddening! I saw Penny pushing her nose up, delighted with the game, but thwarted! Of course Jeannie never held out for more than a moment or two; and then followed quiet munching, a shuffle on the ancient cobble floor of donkey's hooves, and a sense of unbelievable peacefulness on our part.

That Christmas Eve we also had someone else present. I had piled hay at one end of the barn and, in order to keep it away from the donkeys, I had placed an old field gate across it; and on this evening I suddenly caught sight in the candlelight the face of Ambrose, sitting upright in the hay, intrigued by the proceedings, watching us, making me have a silly thought that he looked like a cherub.

It was a starlight night, and when at five to twelve Jeannie and I left the barn, I said to Jeannie it was the most perfect Christmas Eve ceremony ever, and she agreed. And then she said, dashing the moment a little: 'Why, I wonder, did the candle behave like that?'

On Christmas Day, a Thursday, we meandered around Minack, strolled up the lane with Oliver and Ambrose, not too far because we don't want to encourage them to go too far from Minack. Then afterwards we went on our own down to the cliff meadows to see how the spikes of the daffodils were showing. It was a happy, satisfying Christmas Day, ending with a gourmet cooked turkey by Jeannie. One of those days when we say to each other how lucky we are to live a life of such happiness.

I took time to get up next morning. Oliver and Ambrose had spent the night on the bed, cramping me, and when in the morning they jumped off, I lay there, stretching my legs in comfort. It was Jeannie, looking through the window towards the stable field where we had left the donkeys the night before, who caused me to throw the bed-clothes back and dash to get dressed. She had seen the outline of Penny lying flat on the field.

Within three minutes we were beside her. Her eyes were alert enough, but she showed no wish to get up; and so I started to heave her up, heave, heave, until she suddenly decided to struggle to her feet. She stood quite still, and when I tried to get her to walk, she only shuffled a few steps. Once again I hurried off to telephone the vet and, once again, the vet uncomplainingly, despite it being Boxing Day, came out to inspect her. He gave her an injection and told us to continue with the same treatment, douching her feet often with cold water.

She appeared to improve during the day, though she continued to walk very slowly, but when night fell we felt much happier. She had shown a good appetite and, except for her walk, had quite a lively air about her. We had been indoors for an hour, had just watched the TV news, when we heard a car drive up. An unexpected car at night is always unnerving; and I went outside into the dark wondering who on earth it could be.

To my surprise it was David Napper, Jenny's son who, she had told us, was spending Christmas with his own family way up the country. He followed me indoors, sat down, and began talking as if he took it for granted that we had heard the news.

'Don't you know,' he said at last, realising that we were ignorant, 'that Mother has died?'

Jenny . . . Penny . . . the moment flashed through my mind when, years before, we christened the donkeys after Jenny and her Fred.

'I can't believe it!'

'She had a fall. She was found at the bottom of the stairs, clutching in her hand a little box with a white camellia.'

'That's what I gave her!' said Jeannie.

The happiness of Christmas vanished.

'I didn't know that,' David said, 'but I know she was very fond of you.'

He went away soon afterwards, saying he would keep in touch; and we ourselves thanked him for coming to see us, despite all the matters he had to attend to.

Jenny . . . Penny . . . that night, and the following days, those two names were intertwined in our minds. And then came New Year's Eve.

In the morning Penny looked in a bad way. She shuffled her feet inch by inch along the ground; and what also distressed us was that she kept shuffling back to the same place, a place at the far end of the meadow from the barn, close to the hedge which overlooked the field where Fred was born. Thus I would coax her back close to the barn, and then inevitably she would begin a shuffling return. Fred himself was puzzled. He kept near to her, and two or three times I saw him push his nose against her neck, as if he were saying that she was surely not as bad as she appeared to be.

At mid-day the vet was with us again and, he was in high fettle because it was New Year's Eve, and he was going out to dinner that night and was taking a couple of days off. His good humour, needless to say, did not interfere with his concern for Penny.

He repeated that she was suffering from a severe attack of laminitis, and that we should go on with the cold water treatment. He also gave her an injection of cortisone, and also one of another drug; and then, aware of our anxiety, he said he would also prescribe for her a pain killing drug called Phenylbutazone which, I have learnt since, is known in horse circles, particularly horse jumping circles, as *Bute*.

The vet explained that it was important that the drug, which came in the form of a powder in a sachet, should be completely consumed by Penny, adding the suggestion that we might have to use a devious method to succeed in doing this.

Devious method . . . I was told the powders would be ready in the afternoon; and so, as I drove into Penzance to the vet headquarters to collect the powders, Jeannie set out to bake a sponge cake. Penny, she knew, loved sponge cakes, and so she thought if she mixed the powder in the cake, Penny would be sure to consume it.

At 5 pm, and at a time when Penny seemed much more at ease, even walking instead of shuffling, an improvement which we put down to the injections of the vet, we gave Penny her sponge cake. She ate every crumb of it, and we were delighted.

'Oh, I am so glad,' said Jeannie. 'We really have helped her to get on the mend now.'

We went indoors and settled down for a quiet evening; and after about an hour a strange thing happened. Jenny had sent us a Christmas card, a colourful old-fashioned one, and we had placed it on one of the shelves of the dresser. Suddenly it fell off the shelf.

I said nothing for a while, frightened. Then Jeannie broke the silence.

'That's a sign,' she said. 'Jenny is looking after Penny.'

She was wanting to be hopeful, I realised that, and so I didn't reply.

We had supper, saying little.

Then suddenly, as we sat there together, there was a banshee cry outside, no hee-haw, no conventional call from a donkey, but a cry of such an agonising note that it sent a chill right through me.

I rushed into the porch and opened the door, and there was Fred, standing there, shouting his message at us that he needed us; and not thinking how he could possibly have come to the door, knowing that the gate was shut (later we discovered he had jumped the four feet drop from the bank beside the gate), we rushed down with the torch to the stable field, and found Penny at the far end lying on her side. She was breathing heavily.

All night Jeannie stayed with her while Fred kept within a few yards, coming close every now and then, nosing her. It was a clear night at first, stars peaceful companions; and as Jeannie knelt there, a rug over Penny, Jeannie stroking and whispering to her, I again had dashed off to telephone . . . New Year's Eve and the world rejoicing, paper hats and laughter, and noisy bands, and the singing of Auld Lang Syne . . . and when I reached the kiosk at Sheffield and rang up the vet on duty, I told him about the *Bute* powder.

'Give her half as much next time,' he said, as if there would be a next time.

Rain began to fall in the early morning, and I fetched the tarpaulin which covered the tractor, and laid it over Penny; and then Jeannie said it didn't stop the rain falling on her head, and so I collected Jeannie's umbrella, and we opened it, and fixed it over Penny's head; and all the while Fred stayed within a few yards. It is extraordinarily moving to witness the love of one animal for another.

But Fred had sensed, as we knew, that Penny's time was up. She had come the long way from the Connemara Hills to Minack, given much pleasure to many, and her life was over.

Three hours before the service for Jenny Napper was

due to begin at Paul Church, the old church above Mouse-hole, Penny died.

On quiet Sunday evenings we can hear the bells of Paul Church at Minack.

EIGHT

We had no wish to tell anyone. No wish to tell our families, or close friends, or those with whom we were in regular contact. The news had to be kept secret, closeted in our minds, and by so doing we were foolish to pretend that the end of Penny still belonged to us.

Comfortable to cherish illusions in such a situation. The tearing sense of loss seemed to dim in the absence of her being talked about, gossiped about . . . 'Did you hear the Tangyes' donkey is dead?' . . . or perhaps, more sympathetically . . . 'I remember that first birthday party of Fred, and Penny carrying the children on rides, and the shouts of the children . . . can I have a ride? Can I?'

Thus keeping the news eased, in some strange way, our distress. Nothing odd about this. Through the ages those who have loved have been selfish about the news of death.

Yet we needed help and, without demanding anything from us, aware of the sadness, our old friend Walter Grose, the pied piper of cats, and Jack Cockram took command, and time off from their work. Thanks to them, it was organised that Penny was buried in the corner of the stable field, where she used to stand when the southerlies blew, bottom to the wind, sheltered by the corner hedge. She was buried on the Saturday morning.

That evening, as dusk was falling, I was startled by

the sound of a clanging noise a minute or so without stopping, coming from the little yard in front of the barn I was in the small greenhouse, and I did not immediately react. I knew what caused the sound. It was caused when one of the donkeys walked on the metal slide which we used sometimes to block up the gap to the stable field when we wanted the donkeys to stay in the yard; and when I heard the clanging I presumed that Fred was walking on it.

The slide, I must now tell, has sentimental memories for us. Its purpose is the transportation of rocks. You manoeuvre a large rock on it, and then pull it away by tractor; and this particular slide belonged to Jimmy Williams, the legendary Elephant Bill of the XIV Army, who wrote one of the finest of the post-war war books. He was a very dear man, of great sensitiveness, and possessed an extraordinary affinity with animals of all kinds. He had too the capacity of friendship, the subtle patience if a friend on some occasion did not measure up to expectations, the awareness of human frailty, and the imagination to offer his understanding unobtrusively when it was most needed.

He lived at Menwinnion, the rambling house with wooded gardens a mile and a half away from us, over-looking the Lamorna valley, and which is now a hotel, the hotel to which we had walked Penny and Fred. It was in the last summer of his life that he let us have the slide, a leftover tool from the time he had a farm not far from Land's End; and it was that same summer, early that summer, that Monty of *A Cat in the Window* died. We did not know Jim long, only a few months, but it was one of those friendships which is instantly complete, the meeting of minds that does not need time to cement. After he died we became close friends of Sue, his wife, and we introduced her to a publisher, the same publisher who published, at our instigation, *The Cry of a Bird*, the story by Dorothy Yglesias of the Mousehole Bird Hospital; and Sue wrote *Footprints of Elephant Bill*.

But the moment we will remember of Jim, especially Jeannie, was the day after Monty had died, a time when we scarcely knew Jim.

She was in Boots in Penzance, standing beside a counter quite early in the morning, when she heard a voice close to her, saying gently: 'Why are you looking so sad?'

It was Jim, who had watched her, and who had the intuition, and thereby gave her comfort.

But now there was this clanging on the slide and, worrying about Fred, worrying what he might be up to, I hurried out of the small greenhouse and to the yard. To my surprise, I found Jeannie there.

'Where's Fred?' I said.

Jeannie pointed to a far corner of the field.

'Over there.'

'But I heard a clanging . . . as if he were walking on the slide.'

The slide I then saw was lying flat on the ground just opposite the barn door.

'That's what I heard!' she said. 'I heard it indoors, so loud was it, and that's why I came running out!'

Both of us were silent. Was it Penny's ghost?

We saw no one on the Sunday, kept Fred company for much of the day because, during the night, we had been woken up by his trumpeting. I had got out of bed, put on my dressing gown, and gone out to find him; and I had found him by the gate, head over the bar, welcoming the light I shone on him.

On the Monday morning I had to go to St Buryan, and I met Kenny the blacksmith, and I told him the news, and he didn't say anything, just stared at me. He had known Penny since first she came to Minack, and the news hurt him, no doubt about that. But when an animal dies, a human being is hurt in other ways. An era is over; the news makes people feel older.

In the afternoon we had a touching experience. A car drew up outside the cottage, and I cursed, saying to

Jeannie that the last thing I wanted to do was to have to talk to a stranger. It wasn't, however, a stranger. It was a schoolteacher of St Buryan School, who had been present at Fred's birthday parties, and when she saw me she pushed into my hands a large envelope, then hurried back into the car, and drove away.

I was foolish enough not to guess what might be inside the envelope. I thought perhaps she had brought some request for us to do something for the school; and though I thanked her for bringing it to us, I was reserved. Nor did the fact of her hurrying away raise my suspicions. I took the envelope, went back inside the cottage, had a word or two with Jeannie, and sat down. Then I casually opened the envelope.

A small cascade of letters fell out. They came from the children of Class Three, St Buryan School. They were addressed to Fred. A cascade of sympathy.

On the Tuesday another car, a taxi, arrived. It had stopped at Monty's Leap, and a young man got out and came walking up towards the cottage; and when he saw me he asked: 'Are you Derek Tangye?' And when I said yes, he replied: 'My newspaper has sent me to interview you, to do an article about you.'

I panicked. The newspaper has heard about Penny . . . the news will be published, a paragraph announcing it, the bare fact, no hint of our personal distress.

'Wait a minute,' I said, and I left him standing in front of the cottage, and rushed back to Jeannie, who had remained in the cottage.

'A journalist!' I said. 'A young man who has come a long way specially to interview me!'

'Strange coincidence.'

'That's what I'm thinking. A good story for him . . . the death of one of the only two donkeys who ever received a salute from the Q.E.2.'

I was referring to the time when the then captain of the Q.E.2 wrote that he would like to visit us, but he would have to bring the Q.E.2 too. It was during the period when she was calling at Cobh in Eire, then sailing around Land's End to Southampton; and so, at the appointed hour, with Jeannie's clothes line prop stuck in the ground and an orange tablecloth attached to the top as a marker, the Q.E.2 slowly sailed past ... her siren sounding, and on the mainland two donkeys, Penny and Fred, hooting in reply. A memorable occasion.

'Now,' I said, gathering my thoughts together, the young man continuing to wait outside the cottage, 'leave it all to me. Whatever questions he asks let me do the answering unless you get the nod from me.'

'What sort of nod?'

Strange what a diversion can do to ease sadness. Here we were faced with the prospect of Penny's death being publicised, and I was being stimulated by the situation.

'I'll turn to you, and ask you a leading question, and you'll know by my tone whether to answer yes or no.'

'I'll do my best.'

'All right then, I'll go and fetch him.'

I had no idea at that moment how I was going to deal with him. I had, however, been schooled as a reporter on national newspapers and so, in this moment of personal crisis, I was going to rely on my experience. It promised to be interesting, the meeting between my kind of reporter and the new kind.

A reporter, more often than not, has to behave like a confidence trickster. He has to persuade people to be gullible by endearing himself to them, making them believe at a period when they are at their most vulnerable, that they can trust him. Time and again, when I was a reporter in Manchester and London, I behaved this way ... until gradually my triumphs in such deception turned sour, and I escaped.

I now had to act in reverse. I now had to set out to capture the trust of the reporter, making him feel so at home, and myself so willing a co-operator, that he would believe every word I said, or not said. Of course, at that particular moment, before I charmingly invited him into the cottage, I had no certain knowledge that he had arrived because of Penny . . . but I presumed that if he had come to do an article about me, he would certainly know about Penny and Fred and so, finding that Penny had died a couple of days before, he had a story to tell.

I decided that my role should be that of the calm Derek Tangye; and so, after offering him a glass of white wine, I gently began asking questions about himself. How long had he been a reporter? What were his ambitions? How did he view the standard of journalism today? Then gradually I came round to the reason of his visit, and I fished for knowledge about Jeannie and myself. Yes, he said, he had bought the paperback of *The Way to Minack* on the station before catching the train . . . and the information set me back. This meant, without doubt, that he *knew* about Penny and Fred.

It was at the instant of my realising this that another complication arose. I heard the sound of Fred hooting. He was some distance from the cottage, that I knew, but surely, I thought with disquiet, the sound was certain to prompt the reporter to ask about the donkeys.

He did not do so. Nor did he proceed to ask, to my surprise and satisfaction, any questions about the content of *The Way to Minack*, a book which gives in some detail how we came to live our kind of life at Minack. Instead, I soon realised that, despite the fact he had come to write an article about me, he had not even flirted with his homework.

Thus the first question he asked, an old chestnut as far as I was concerned, was: 'When did you come to Minack?'

I have a simple answer to this question, hating time as I do, believing too much emphasis is on age and time, in this flashing age of speed.

'Yesterday,' is my answer.

For an hour and more we continued to talk, commenting

on the manners of today, of youth's ambitions, of politics and any other subject which was as far away as I could get from the subject of ourselves . . . and periodically in the distance I heard Fred hooting.

Eventually he said it was time for him to go and, after seeing him into his taxi, I hurried back to Jeannie.

'A miracle,' I said. 'He had never even heard of the donkeys!'

Jeannie was looking out of the window.

'Don't be so sure,' she said. 'The taxi has stopped at the entrance of the field where Fred is . . . and the man's coming back.'

But there was no cause for us to be anxious.

'I forgot,' said the young man when he reached us, 'to ask whether a photographer could come tomorrow to illustrate my article.'

Of course, with relief, we agreed; and the photographer duly arrived, took his photographs, and then he too departed without mentioning the donkeys.

A month later the article appeared in a weekend newspaper, the reporter's eye view of life at Minack, and not a word about the donkeys . . . and in heavy black type the following sentence about Minack:

NOTHING TERRIBLE EVER HAPPENS.

We smiled when we read it. It did us good. We had had luck on our side, and we had made full use of it, and full use of past experience. We had duped the reporter. We had kept our mouths shut when others, without the knowledge of journalists, would have prattled. And of course the luck on our side was that the reporter had never done his homework. Dear Penny, he had never heard of her.

I look back on our own times in London, however, and have sympathy with such people. A city life, surrounded by cement, deafened by noise, made harsher every day by ever decreasing living standards, compelled to queue for whatever transport is available, chased by competing office colleagues, heavy lunches and stress-making conferences . . . such factors inevitably numb the brain.

My own media period covered the Beaverbrook and Rothermere era. These were robber baron days. The proprietors and their editors acted on whims, prejudices, envy of each other, and the need to maintain perpetual excitement. It was infectious. Reporters caught the scent of a story and followed it to the end without thought of the overtime involved, the lack of payment for such overtime, and the fact that the security of their jobs was often wafer-thin. For that was a special aspect of the robber baron days. A reporter could be a hero one day, then fired the next, for no apparent reason except that the editor had suddenly grown tired of his face. Dangerous days, but it was fun, a young man's fun at any rate.

The most important lesson I learnt in those days of being a reporter concerned intuition. I learnt that, however mentally equipped a person might be, however distinguished his professional qualifications might be, he was arid without intuition. The essence of intuition is awareness of a situation which logic tells you does not exist; like the intuition of a brilliant three quarter on the rugby football field. He weaves his way through the opposing side, dashing this way and that, following no rule book, led by his intuition as to how to pierce the defence. A brilliant business tycoon operates in similar fashion, so does a politician, detective, publisher, or jockey, or anyone else who is above the crowd. Intuition, however, cannot be taught. Governments cannot legalise it on the grounds that we should all be equal. People are born with intuition, like a horse who is born with the quality to win the Derby. Intuition is a gift. Fortunately for us, the reporter who came to Minack didn't have it.

We now began to ease out of our sadness, the repairing period had begun, no longer was it a continuous pain, the pain instead came in sudden moments, when waking up in the morning, believing for an instant that the world was as it always has been, then suddenly realising that Penny was not there waiting for us; and it came in the evening when darkness had fallen, and we had given Fred his feed of hay, and we left him to spend the night alone. Legions, every day, feel as we did, sorrow which reaches into the secret heart, cherished in a way because it is a memorial to love shared.

Jeannie and I also had other matters on our minds, and these helped to divert us. The honeymoon of being without Geoffrey, of being on our own without manual work to be done, was at an end. The dormant winter months were over, the daffodil season was on the verge of beginning, and I had to face the fact that the tasks taken care of by Geoffrey had now to be done by myself. I had to put the first vision into practice. No longer could I nostalgically talk about it. I had to act.

Clearly we could not continue with the same growing output as before. We could reasonably manage the daffodil season provided the weather was not warm, thus bringing the blooms on too fast, because we could draw on extra help, Margaret Smith, for instance, who works the pottery at the end of the lane with her husband. But the growing of tomatoes on the same scale as before was out of the question. We could not possibly look after three thousand tomato plants by ourselves because of the hand labour involved. Nor, judging from the previous season when Geoffrey spent most of his time looking after them, and we only received a few hundred pounds in return for the wages and the other costs, making a considerable loss, was it financially worth while even to contemplate doing so. Thus we decided that, for the first year on our own, we would have a token number of tomato plants, a hundred or so, and grow them without heat in the Orlyt greenhouse below the cottage. Even so, we realised, because of the climate in the west of Cornwall, we could plant them in the middle of March, and catch the market before the main cold crop came in. A hundred plants, pathetically few compared with other years, but there was the chance not to make a loss. It could prove to be another example of small being beautiful.

Such a decision, however, meant that the other four greenhouses, each seventy feet long and twenty feet wide, would be empty. I decided, therefore, to have an original crop in two of them, original as far as we ourselves were concerned, and the crop I had in mind was carrots. Early carrots, the year before, even those grown in the open, had earned a lot of money; and so, I thought, if we grew carrots in the greenhouse, we might hit the jackpot.

This optimistic notion, I realised much later, had a whiff of our first vision, because an essential ingredient of the first vision was our unbounded optimism. We had the bright idea one summer, for instance, to sell daffodil bulbs in packs. Today, of course, there are bulb packs galore on sale, but we were the first among Cornish growers to think of the idea. We believed we were about to make our fortune, bought twenty thousand specially designed polythene bags, feverishly filled them with the bulbs we equally feverishly dug out of the ground, rushed them around to shops . . . and waited. We were before our time. The following summer the big boys moved in, and swamped the market. As for ourselves, we still have nineteen thousand of the polythene bags stacked in the barn.

Thus two of the greenhouses were assigned to Early Nantes carrots, four ounces in all and, although this would produce a great number of carrots, the outlay was insignificant. We were determined to avoid outlay. We were tired of backing crops in the same way as punters back outsiders with money they cannot afford. Carrots, therefore, were a sensible programme for us, possibly highly profitable . . . and, in any case, food for Fred.

We labelled these two carrot houses C and D. There were also, however, greenhouses A and B. I was doubtful what to do with these until Jeannie suggested that we use them for our personal purposes . . . and this meant that A would be devoted to a mingling of growing cucumbers, sweet peas, marrows and winter chrysanthemums, while B was left to continue growing the Cape Gooseberries. They had been growing there for the past two years. Originally grown from seed, they were cut down to within twelve inches of the ground at the end of each fruiting season. An easy crop to grow, and my only job would be to keep them weeded.

We had, therefore, a growing pattern to follow during the coming months; a pattern which seemed simple enough in theory, but which did not include the trickiest of my problems . . . machinery and maintenance.

There was, for example, the task of dealing with panes of glass in the greenhouses, splintered into pieces by the gales. Already I had had experience of this, and I did not enjoy it. True, it had been remarkable the way the greenhouses had stood up to ferocious gales but, as they began to age, weaknesses developed. Periodically, while the gales blew, I would gingerly walk round the outside of the greenhouses to see whether any damage had occurred, and twice in recent weeks I had found smashed glass on the ground, and the gale blowing through the open frame, threatening to do even greater damage.

Jeannie ordered me not to attempt any repairs while the gale blew, but I disobeyed. I was too concerned about the risk of the greenhouse being shattered to be worried about myself. The repair work was also easier than it looked. It would, of course, have been impossible to use glass, to carry a large sheet of glass, and to try to fix it in position in a gale; but now the job was simplified by the remarkable horticultural polythene, the correct size to cover the frame which I cut from a roll, and then fixed it into position by stamping numerous staples through the polythene into the wooden frame. Simplified it may have been, but the prospect of plugging gaps in the greenhouse whenever a gale blew was not one I looked forward to with enjoyment.

There was too the general maintenance of the twenty acres of land, the trimming of hedges, the cutting of the bracken that covers the bulb meadows down the cliff at summer's end, and the cutting of the grass in the fields, and all the other humdrum work that Geoffrey performed, leaving me time to write and to meet people.

Then there was the machinery, the Leyland tractor I had never regularly driven, and the rotovator I had forgotten how to use, and the formidable rotary grass and undergrowth cutting machine which Geoffrey always seemed to have trouble to get started. I was a novice in such matters, and I would have to be careful. Once, early on at Minack, the rotovator I was driving upset and a tine pierced my foot, and I was hobbling with a stick for weeks.

Problems concerning oneself, however, tend to enlarge themselves if one does not keep them under strict control. Thus I have found that it is best, having added up the problems so that I know exactly what has to be faced, to relax. Deal with those that are immediate, but do not strain after the others. If I haven't time to deal with them, don't chase them.

There was also another factor in my calculations. I was indulging in what I wanted to do, in the environment I wanted to live in, and Jeannie and I were enjoying a life that so many others would have loved if they had had the luck. Problems we had, yes, but they were problems of our own making. They were not being forced upon us by unions or employers. They were created solely by ourselves. In a community minded age, we wanted to be on our own. And we were.

But, during this period when we were planning the future, Fred was hooting. In the middle of the night, or just when we were going to bed, or at first light, or in the middle of a rainy day, Fred would sear the countryside with his sad hoots.

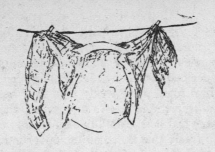

NINE

We should perhaps have set out immediately to find another donkey to be a companion for Fred. Many people in similar circumstances would have done so, no doubt, and logically they may have been right.

Two factors, however, stopped us. One was sentiment. Neither of us could bear the thought of seeing another donkey gambolling about the meadows so soon. In time, yes, but for the present we refused to entertain the idea of looking for such a donkey. We were impelled to remain loyal for a while to the memory of Penny. It was a form of the old fashioned custom of going into mourning. It is not a question of going around with a long face. It is just a question of having a pause between the old and the new. No haste to find a substitute for the one who has given you love for years. Wait, and let fate provide the answer.

The second factor, and it was a realistic one, was the advice given to us by an experienced donkey owner. He said that a donkey will sometimes reject angrily a strange donkey which has been provided as a replacement. He advised that a donkey such as Fred, who had known no other donkey all his life except his mother, might well attack the stranger; and he advised that it would be sensible if we waited until his memory of her dimmed.

An antidote, meanwhile, had to be found for his loneliness. Something, obviously, had to be done to occupy his mind, some new routine, some new adventure to enjoy, and so we decided that the wisest thing we could do would be to let him roam more freely than ever before. There had always been the meadows to roam in, acres of them, but the gates had been carefully shut to stop the donkeys roaming so freely that they had the opportunity to demolish the garden. I had no intention of allowing Fred, under the new plan we were about to implement, to demolish the garden . . . but we were prepared to let him roam loose while we were ourselves in the garden's vicinity.

Within a short time, however, there were complications. Obviously he enjoyed his new freedom, and we would watch him happily munching the grass in the small orchard.

'How good,' I would innocently say to Jeannie, 'to see Fred happy again!'

Such a sentiment lulled us. We stopped watching him, deserted our jobs as supervisors, and allowed him to go about his roaming business unobserved. We were treating him like Oliver and Ambrose. This was a donkey who could be trusted.

It was not so.

'Fred!'

I heard Jeannie's cry one morning when I was indoors, and I immediately hurried outside.

'Look what he's done!'

Jeannie was pointing to the stumps of two saplings.

'Never mind,' I said.

'But they're finished!'

'We'll get two more.'

Fred had devoured the plum trees planted the previous autumn.

Jeannie, of course, was not as upset as she had first appeared. We both realised that this plan to give Fred his freedom entailed risks. There was a veronica bush, for instance, for which he had a fancy, and this in due course became a bush of sticks instead of a bush of leaves. But my attitude on these occasions of destruction remained static. Any demolition was worth it if Fred was helped to take his mind off the fact that he was now alone.

Sometimes when he was roaming, he would come up the path and round the corner of the cottage to the porch. If we were indoors, we would hear him softly snorting, and we would leap to the door, and welcome him, and find a chocolate biscuit, and if there were no chocolate biscuits, we could cut a slice off Jeannie's home-made bread; and Fred would munch it with enjoyment, and we would talk to him, and stroke his head, and then, when he had had enough both of the bread and of our attention, he would turn his bottom to us and wander off. I would watch him, and think what a beautiful donkey he was, the coat of deep chestnut and a way of carrying himself like a thoroughbred polo pony. Heaven knows what his father was like, a hard working Irish tinker's donkey, Jeannie always likes to think, but both he and Penny shared the very fine characteristics of the traditional Spanish donkey which, in the last century, was introduced into Ireland.

Other misfortunes, misfortunes from our point of view, were soon to take place after the departure of the plum saplings and the veronica bush. In pursuit of keeping him amused, we took Fred one day to the field beside the winding lane which we call the greenhouse field; and having led him there, having put a wooden plank across the entrance which is close to Monty's Leap, we departed, lulled again by the sight of him wandering off happily among the grassy beds of California daffodils.

'Are you absolutely sure he won't damage them?' said Jeannie, the period being early February, and the California harvest time due within a couple of weeks.

'I'm sure he won't,' I said, nonchalantly, 'and anyhow what is a lost California or two if Fred is keeping the grass down?'

However, as it turned out, the California daffodils,

long stems, a cup of yellow, scented, and sometimes called Pentewan, were not going to be the subject of Fred's next escapade.

I had foolishly left the door open of one of the greenhouses growing our early carrots.

Thus it was my turn to cry out when, later in the day, I went to see how Fred was getting on. Getting on? He had walked through the open door of the greenhouse, and indulged in his most luxurious indulgence . . . a roll, and another roll, and another roll in the newly cultivated soft earth; and the carrot seed on the chosen spot had been obliterated.

Fred also, as time went by, had other diversions which had nothing to do with any effort on our part to provide them. There were the escaping steers, for instance.

This was the herd of steers belonging to the absentee farmer on the other side of the western boundaries of Minack which had already invaded us. The farmer himself lived in a farm many miles away, and so the steers were relied upon to behave themselves in his absence. They didn't. And, on this occasion when they broke out over our boundary, bursting through a hedge and pummelling aside the barbed wire which was there to stop them, it was Fred who alerted us that they were on the rampage.

I saw him in the stable meadow, ears pointed, head so absorbed at what he saw happening at the other end of the stable meadow, on the other side of the hedge in the big field where he was born, that I instantly realised what must have occurred.

I raced down the path to the white gate which shut off the stable meadow from Fred's field, and Fred careered along with me. He adored this sudden excitement. He wanted to prolong it, he wanted to join the herd of steers, which I now found were devouring the leaves of the ollearia, and trampling on the green spikes of the daffodils, daffodils which were just beginning to show their buds.

Fred, at this moment, was free, no memories, no

loneliness . . . I had, however, to stop him from the pleasure he truly would have enjoyed. I could not rely on him to behave in the manner of a sheepdog, helping me to round up the wandering steers, and drive them back whence they came. I had, therefore, to shut the gate, leaving him to look over it disconsolately, while I set off with stick in hand, the steers stampeding ahead of me, until I corralled them in our boundary field, fixed a barricade to stop them returning, then hurried up to the farm, borrowed my neighbour's telephone, and told the absentee farmer what had happened.

The man had already had troubles with these steers. They had trampled a neighbouring garden, and he had to pay out compensation. I myself might have demanded compensation for the bruised daffodil bulbs and the devoured hedges, but a countryman is not quick on the mark. It might happen to him in reverse. His cattle, or his donkeys, might be doing the damage next week. And, in any case, the owner of these steers was always co-operative; and he showed it in special measure when, without any request from me, he arrived one day with a number of ollearia rooted cuttings which he had acquired specially from the Forestry Commission's plantations near Lostwithiel.

We had Margaret Smith, the potter at the end of the lane, to help us during the daffodil season. Margaret and George, her husband, were Londoners who came to live in Cornwall several years ago. Their pottery is both practical and beautiful, and we have several of their pieces, including the teapot in which I make the morning tea. They have two pretty daughters, Jenny who is a schoolteacher, and Nina who has been studying graphics, and a son who is an apprentice in the Penzance ship repairing yard. Both Jenny and Nina sometimes helped at weekends when the daffodil season was at its height.

Margaret herself was an enthusiast, indefatigable, with legions of friends, and so easy a manner that it enhanced the day to have her working alongside us . . . and Fred. Fred had a special liking for her and, for some particular reason, he seemed to have a special liking for a brown woolly hat which she wore when the weather was rough. Wandering at will among the daffodil beds, pausing and staring, stepping with remarkable care between the daffodils themselves, he would suddenly espy Margaret and her woolly hat. Thereupon he would cross the daffodil beds, stand beside her as she continued to pick, and then take a bite at the hat. He would not leave her until she had given him a special attention in return.

He was remarkably careful as he walked among the daffodils. Although, when we first decided to allow him to be with us, we were prepared to accept the certainty that he would cause damage, the certainty never occurred. I never found a broken stem of a daffodil where he had walked . . . but if there had been the two of them, if in time past we had let both him and Penny join us in daffodil picking, there would have been trouble. Two donkeys together like to play, and galloping feet would have scattered both foliage and blooms.

Margaret was a compulsive talker. When she and Jeannie went to the end of a row to start picking, and I was at the other end of the row, also picking, I would hear a sound like the hum of bees coming nearer and nearer, punctuated by staccato interruptions of yes and no from Jeannie, until they reached the point where I was picking when we would interchange a few words, then they would pass me, and I would listen to the hum fading into the distance.

Margaret never admitted she was tired. She was ready to go out and pick in all weathers; and sometimes when a gale is blowing, and the rain is lashing your face as if a hose was directed upon you, daffodil picking is an uncomfortable business. Your hands and fingers become numb, and you have to chase the stems as you bend down, because the gale is blowing them this way and that.

Margaret's only problem as far as we were concerned was her devotion to riding. Her enthusiasms included attending classes of meditation, strict vegetarianism, sauna baths, singing, and now riding. She was a soloist in the Lamorna Choir, the choir created by Sampson Hosking, a choir which has a fine reputation in Cornwall.

But riding was the dominant enthusiasm that year of Fred's first daffodil season on his own.

'Will you want me tomorrow afternoon? I've booked my favourite horse at Rosehill. . . .'

Rosehill being the riding stables.

'. . . It doesn't matter. I can cancel if you do.'

And the next day.

'Didn't you get soaked? We thought of you when the heavens opened.'

'Awful, awful . . . but it was fun.'

It was fun too, all through the daffodil season. It was fun to have someone on our side, ready to fit in with any of our plans or emergencies, without feeling a sense of strain. It was fun, too, to wake up as dawn was breaking, and go out and pick, Jeannie and I, knowing that every bloom we picked and bunched was money we were earning for ourselves; and that later, soon after breakfast, Margaret would cheerfully arrive to help us.

This was the first vision . . . the idyllic present, freedom from employer responsibility, being absorbed by one's own hard work, undeterred by long hours because one was being exhilarated by one's own achievement. Bunches of daffodils which would give pleasure to homes in city streets. Pride in the contents of every daffodil box we despatched. Satisfaction at the day's end. Crossing our fingers that our luck would hold. The luck of being able to live the kind of life we loved.

Each of us, no one will stop me from believing, is ruled by luck, and not by logic. The intellect can plan, analyse, conjure up alternative moves, create computer programmes to foretell future contingencies . . and the outcome of such plans is still dependent on luck. Life would be dull if it weren't. If we were all at the mercy of logic, there would be no carrot to motivate our lives. Those bored by their daily routine would have no dreams to dream about, no chance of surprise meetings, or winning a football pool, or a miracle happening . . . everything pre-planned, everything neatly computerised, no risks, no unexpected pleasures, always safe. I can hear the yawns.

Yet there is a snag about my beliefs. How does one recognise luck when it comes in the form of opportunity? Material luck is obvious, but opportunity tends to be obscure. Hence there have been many times in my life when I have looked back on an opportunity missed, and wondered why I missed it. The opportunity is crystal clear years later, and yet at the time I fumbled, and lost it. Why? If you keep a diary it will help to explain, and I have always kept a diary from time to time but not regularly, because, as Virginia Woolf said, diaries should only be kept at intervals, otherwise the diary dominates the diarist. What, then, has my diary to tell me about lost opportunities?

I find, for instance, that my memory over-simplifies the moment when the opportunity was presented. At the distance of time, it appears bewildering that I did not seize it, there it was staring at me in the face, so what idiocy stopped me from taking it? But I read my diary, and find the answer, part of the answer at any rate.

It is that opportunities seem to present themselves when the mind is muddled by conflicting circumstances, intensely real at the time, but which fade into oblivion as the years pass. Thus the picture of the opportunity remains in the mind, but not its frame. I find, therefore, in my diary that my mood at the time often did not fit the opportunity, and also that timidity has played a part in my lost opportunities, an unwillingness to risk a rebuke; and I find that often I would believe the circumstances around the opportunity could be more perfect, so I would wait, as if I were waiting for the starting gun of a race, and then I would find the opportunity was no longer there. I find also that I sometimes have fallen into the trap of adding up the pros and cons of an opportunity, adding them up again and again, until, with my spirit of adventure drained from me, I opted for the comfort of playing safe.

On the other hand, there have been those occasions when I have seized my opportunities and, as I see in my diary, these all have a common pattern. I have allowed my instinct to take charge. I have avoided sensible deliberation, and have acted quickly before the danger of second thoughts. An old story of letting the heart have its freedom, instead of the head its calculating coolness.

Three such occasions . . . the first was when I wrote a well-publicised column for the *Daily Mirror*. There I was, young, a bachelor, fêted like a pop star ('Calm, girls, calm yourselves' called out the photographer when I visited the Hammersmith Palais), handing out money raised by my readers to other readers less fortunate ('I've stolen from the petty cash of the shop where I work. I'll never do it again. Can you help? Five pounds I need'); and then one morning, I arrived at the office with tickets booked that evening for a tour of European capitals . . . and I was greeted by a note to see the editor. I was no longer needed. I was fired. It was then that my instinct took charge. Here, I said to myself, was my chance to go round the world; and I committed myself immediately by asking the editor if I could write one last column . . . and I wrote that I was giving up my column in order to get away from it all, and to seek adventure when I was still young. That seized opportunity, I am sure, saved my life; and for a reason I will not go into now.

The second occasion was when I proposed to Jeannie. I had been waiting for her for over an hour at the Coal Hole, the pub in the Strand close to the Savoy Hotel. She had been delayed in the American Bar, entertaining American war correspondents . . . and when she at last arrived to meet me, she brought as a peace offering a bottle of Savoy whisky. I put it aside, showing no enthusiasm, and she was surprised. She was even more surprised when, instead of thanking her, I said: 'Will you marry me?'

The third occasion was when both of us decided we would leave our London life, and start a new one at Minack. Had we paused to think, had we considered the risk we ran, had we painstakingly checked upon the problems facing us about making a living from the land, if we had behaved sanely, we would not have been at Minack today.

Fred had another diversion during the daffodil season; a friendship he developed with a cow which belonged to Jack Cockram. The scene of the love affair began at the wire fence which separates the Lama field from that of the lush grass where Jack's cattle grazed, the Lama field being just above the bridge where we spend many hours, too many idle hours, staring across the moorland at the sea of Mount's Bay.

On one side of the fence would stand Fred, knee-deep among the daffodil foliage, and on the other side, a nose away, stood the cow, a pretty Guernsey cow. All the other cows of the herd would wander off, grazing elsewhere, but Fred's cow would continue to remain faithful to Fred. They communed together. Clearly they were very attached to each other. Perhaps, for all I know, they were sharing an experience . . . Fred having lost Penny, the cow her calf to the market. Have you ever heard at night the cry of a cow after her calf has been taken away? For me, when I hear the sound, I always remember the hoots of Fred after Penny died.

Donkeys, many farmers believe, have a good effect on a herd of cows, even believing that the presence of a donkey on a farm prevents miscarriages among the cows; the kind of country belief like the one about the adder and the ash tree . . . if you are bitten by an adder, hasten to an ash, huddle close to it, and the adder's poison will bring you no harm. The problem, however, find the ash.

Apart from the wire fence, stone hedges separated Jack's herd from Fred and, though a Cornish hedge is solidly built, it is also very ancient and, inevitably, as the years go by, weaknesses develop, and these weaknesses are the source of much pleasure to bored cows, or bored donkeys. Fred's cow, for instance, was clever in exploiting them. She would nose around the neighbouring field, find a weakness, paw at it until the stones had further weakened, then heave herself up and over, to be greeted by a welcoming Fred.

Soon other cows would follow, and we would suddenly look out of the porch window and find the field above the cottage awash with cows, making me incongruously think of a mass meeting for the Daughters of the American Revolution which I attended once in America. Now that they were in possession of the field, the cows had other places to explore. Sometimes, for instance, they crashed like buffaloes through our little wood, and there was always the risk they could escape further, into the vegetable garden, for example, or, if it were daffodil time, they could cause havoc among the daffodils.

Hence, as soon as they were discovered, I would rush up to the farm and alert Jack as to what his eighty or so ladies were up to and, in due course, he would come down and, after much shouting and running, we would succeed in shepherding the cows back whence they came.

Fred's excursions into *their* land, however, were few and far between. Nor could he threaten the damage that might be done by the cows. If we saw he had escaped, we also saw that he was gently grazing alongside them, for all he was requiring was company. On one occasion, when Penny and Fred had escaped together, and were quietly grazing among the herd, Jack came down to his gate at the regular hour of half past four to call the cows in for milking. The calls alerted Penny and Fred to an imaginary responsibility, for they stopped their grazing, joined the cows, then self-importantly led them across the field, through a gap in the wood, across another field, to the gate where a surprised Jack was waiting. Evidence, in fact, that donkeys are at home on a farm.

Fred, during this time of the daffodil season, had yet another diversion in the form of the arrival of the hunt one day. It was a windy day and we had left Fred in the Q.E.2 meadow where we had spent the early part of the morning picking Hollywood, a prolific, early daffodil; and he was sheltering from the westerly with his bottom to the high hedge at the top of the meadow, his head facing across the valley.

Suddenly, as we were gently bunching the daffodils, we heard shouts, then a tally-ho, then the sound, in the distance but coming nearer, of galloping horses then, drowning all these noises, the trumpeting, hysterical hooting of Fred; the hoot he reserved for occasions of very special excitement.

We hurried to join him, and we saw across the shallow valley, in the top fields belonging to Bill Trevorrow, a line of riders galloping towards the cliff which we knew they could not reach, and the fox knew it, because of the dense gorse, brambles, and undergrowth that barred the way on the other side of the hedge they were galloping towards. Then we saw another rider, who had broken away from the others, come cantering down our lane, reach Monty's Leap, jump it, then suddenly stop as if he had seen an anti-hunt sign, turn round and canter back again. Fred was mad with excitement. He rushed round the field, ears pricked, bellowing his special hoot, rejoicing in this change of his daily routine. His excitement did not last long. The disconsolate riders, having discovered the undergrowth barrier, turned back; and the fox, and we had seen this before on local hunt days, found safety after his long run, in an earth down the cliff, an enviable residence looking out on Mount's Bay, hidden from human's view, except from ourselves who knew where to look.

Yet, I have to admit, that in this imperfect world, I find the hunt a lesser of two evils. A hunt gives a chance for the fox to escape, it gives a chance for horses to live which would otherwise go to the knacker's yard, and it harnesses members of the hunt to join with the rest of us against the worst threat to foxes that can be imagined. Gin traps are the worst threat. Illegal for catching rabbits, but legal for catching foxes.

These gin traps are increasingly in use. The reason is that a trade has developed in fox skins, and the buyers of these skins encourage men to catch the foxes by traps. Shooting is no good because it spoils the skin, and it also awakens the neighbourhood to what is happening. Hence traps are laid in the neighbourhood of fox earths, and it doesn't matter what season of the year it may be. It could be in May when the cubs are around. Nobody cares, provided the fox is caught, skinned, parcelled up and taken to the local post office. Country post offices are intimate concerns, and the postmaster keeps an eye on every local person's affairs. But, though he may disapprove of the traffic in fox skins, though he may be aware who is engaged in this traffic, there is nothing he can do except to post the parcel.

I am, however, conscious of the potential danger that a fox has for a cat. Foxes, individual rogue foxes, but not foxes in general terms, are known to attack cats. People were sipping a pint at the Old Success in Sennen Cove near Land's End one bright Sunday morning, when they saw a fox appear in the car park outside the bar window, seize a local cat by its tail, and dash off with it. The cat escaped after a hundred yards or so, but minus the end of its tail.

Hence I am on guard about Oliver and Ambrose. Not that I am unduly worried about them. I have seen Oliver, for instance, sitting beside a fox in the lane on the other side of Monty's Leap, as if they were having a gossip, and for months Oliver slept in the little house I made for

137

him in the copse near the Leap without harm coming to him.

It is, however, on warm summer nights that I become anxious over their whereabouts. True, they may be ensconced in the Orlyt or the small greenhouse, for we always leave the doors ajar, and they may also be curled up on the sofa or in the spare bedroom . . . but on warm summer nights they have a readiness to sleep out, under the apple tree perhaps, outside our bedroom window, or somewhere else in the grass.

The aftermath of a tragedy can be full of ifs . . . if we hadn't taken the car out, if we hadn't let him go out that evening, if we had called the vet when we first sensed trouble, if, if, if . . . in my case I try to anticipate another if. One evening during the summer, I watched a young fox come into the front garden, sniff around, then crouch, ready to spring at some object which was just out of sight of me. It sprang, then I saw it glide speedily away with a blackbird in its mouth.

Thus it is that I am prepared to rise from my bed in the early hours to search out the sleeping quarters of Oliver and Ambrose; and when I have found them curled in the grass, paws around each other as if they were the babes in the wood, I gather them up, soggy with sleep, and carry them to the Orlyt where, to their later fury, they discover the door is shut. The shut door gives me the chance to sleep peacefully.

Fred, as the daffodil season progressed, and the end of March came, and the holiday season of April began, had therefore his diversions, and the freedom of Minack. Indeed his freedom was such that foolishly we allowed him to roam on the grass where Jeannie's clothes line is hoisted.

'Look!' she called out in dismay one afternoon after she had hung out the washing in the morning.

Fred had chewed off the sleeve of my new shirt.

TEN

April. The holiday season had begun, and now came the questions we were to hear all summer.

'What *did* happen to Penny? Was it her age? How does Fred feel? Are you getting a companion for him soon?'

People who had been here before, people who had only read about them in books, all came with the same questions. We had difficulty in answering them. We didn't wish to put on a special air of solemnity, yet we couldn't be light-hearted. Easy, however, to answer the question about Fred having a companion.

'I am waiting,' I would say, 'for a donkey to come down the lane as if out of nowhere . . . in the manner of Oliver and Ambrose, the miracle cats.'

One lady took me seriously. She returned a couple of days later with the news that she had found a donkey for sale, that she had enquired about hiring a horse-box to transport the donkey and, if I agreed, she would supervise the arrival of the donkey at the top of the lane, where she would direct the donkey down the lane towards Minack. An optimistic lady, who clearly had little knowledge of donkeys. I thanked her, and explained that the donkey was most unlikely to co-operate and, in any case, we didn't want a miracle to happen just yet.

The miracle cats, meanwhile, Oliver the black double

of Lama, Ambrose the rich marmalade double of Monty, were daily being courted by admirers who wished to make their acquaintance. They did not welcome this attention. True, Oliver could occasionally be accommodating, even to the extent of allowing someone to stroke him, but these moments were rare. For the most part, he kept his distance. He would sit on a rock listening to the endearments of an admirer, balefully staring at her, wondering, I feel sure, why human beings, instead of talking normally to cats, always fawn.

Ambrose, on the other hand, never gave anyone the chance to touch him. Magnificent to look at, he despised the human race. He also had an inborn fear of it. It was as if he instinctively knew that the human race is always ready to destroy for the sake of materialism, jettisoning love, beauty, moral principles, if need be; and in that sense cats, useless, non-money making cats, were expendable. Thus he had no use for strangers, however well meaning. He would dash away as soon as they approached, and the only opportunity they would have to see him at close range was after he had had a large meal, and he was dozing, curled up in a hide-out which we first had to find.

Even in his attitude to Jeannie and me, he had his inhibitions. He was affectionate, but only on his own terms. He was not going to be used like a toy, picked up, cuddled, played with, just because the mood to do so suited either of us. Thus I might approach him, bend down to reach him, and he would run away. Oliver would never run away. Oliver was always ready instantly to return love with love.

Yet Ambrose, remote as he sometimes would be, would suddenly show a burst of affection towards me, such as surprisingly coming up to me as I stood on the bridge, rubbing his head against my leg, or jumping onto my lap, as I sat reading on the sofa. He was two years old before he jumped on a lap. We were beginning to despair that he was ever going to condescend to make this customary cat gesture . . . when it happened. Jeannie was sitting opposite me, and she looked astonished, envious too, that I was the first lap to receive the accolade, as Ambrose settled down, overlapping my legs because he was already so large.

He was, however, Jeannie's cat, not mine. It was for Jeannie that he reserved his special attention, and no wonder. Jeannie combed his thick coat, Jeannie provided his meals, Jeannie had an affinity with him that I, despite the fact he chose to jump on to my lap first, didn't seem to have. The affinity with me may develop as the years go by. I hope so. I believe there are signs, other than those I have mentioned, which show promise.

Sleeping on the bed, for instance. As someone who was brought up in a practical family, who thought cats were unclean, and irritating because they did not immediately obey a whistle as a well mannered dog would do, I had to have a long education in order to appreciate that a cat on a bed was an honour. Monty provided me with my primary education, Lama with my comprehensive, Oliver and Ambrose with a rebellious university one. I say rebellious because, when Oliver and Ambrose moved in at Minack, I thumped the breakfast table with my fist on the morning it was suggested by Jeannie that they both might soon be sleeping on the bed. On no account, I declared, though disturbed by the memory that I had used similar language about Monty, then about Lama . . . on no account, I thumped again, would they do so. One cat was understandable, but certainly not two. I long ago surrendered.

One recent night, for instance, I dreamt that a heavy rock had fallen from a high cliff upon my legs, and that debris from the cliff was heaped upon my face, slowly suffocating me, while all around was the roar of the sea. I had one of those battles to wake up and free myself from the dream; and, having done so, I found what constituted the rock, and what constituted the debris. The rock was Ambrose, the debris was Oliver's fur. Ambrose was pinioning my legs at the bottom of the bed, Oliver was lying

144

between my chin and my chest. As for the roar of the sea in my dream, it was the sound of their purrs. Both were purring at full throttle.

Oliver, in contrast with my doubts about Ambrose, loves me. This extraordinary cat, born in a little cave among the daffodil meadows down the cliff, whose mother was Daisy, the grey cat who was Lama's mother too, and who brought him when he could walk up from the cliff to our barn below the cottage, where we used to watch him through the window drinking the milk we left for him, smothering his face in milk when doing so, in exactly the same way that he does today . . . this extraordinary cat, who disappeared one day from the barn, then four years later worked his way back to Minack, sleeping on a hedge for a while, then in a miniature house I built for him in the copse near Monty's Leap, always denied a welcome while Lama was alive, watches me. At unexpected moments he is suddenly beside me.

It was during a period in April when I was wondering why the carrots in the two greenhouses, C and D, were not growing fast enough, that Oliver allowed himself to get into a music hall predicament. I was in one of the greenhouses one morning when I heard a dog barking in the copse by Monty's Leap. I was, however, so absorbed by the carrots, or the lack of them, that I did not take immediate notice. The carrots had been sowed in beds, four rows in each bed, twelve inches between each row, at the beginning of February; and yet here it was April and only a bare scattering of carrots had appeared despite my regular watering, a watering done with my thumb over the hose so as to make a spray. Early Nantes was one variety of carrot I had sown, Amsterdam Forcing was another, but neither were in green rows as they should have been, only patches of green.

I was ruminating about the whys and wherefores when I suddenly realised that my daydreaming had made me deaf to the barks; and I was immediately on the alert. I hurried from the greenhouse down to the lane, calling out all the time to the dog. I could not guess whose dog it could be, but dogs do find their way to Minack, lost ones at that.

The previous year, we had been lucky enough to release a beagle from a vicious badger trap. From early evening we had heard this dog barking in the moorland towards Lamorna; and in the early hours, when we realised it must be in trouble, we went out to search for it. I found it among the bracken, a front paw in the trap and, with Jeannie holding a torch, I was able to cut the wire free from the trap. We could not, however, free the wire around the paw, and so we carried the beagle back to the cottage, got out the car, and set off for Penzance. At four in the morning, I telephoned the vet, and we met him at the surgery, and twenty minutes later the beagle was wagging his tail in freedom.

And, recently, during the daffodil season, we had had an odd experience with a black and white collie. It was a Sunday morning when Jeannie called out that this collie was outside the front door; and she forthwith went into the kitchen and took a meat bone which had been scheduled for the Trevorrow dogs at the top of the lane. She gave the collie the bone, and I disapproved.

'You're silly to do that,' I said. 'It won't go away now.'

I was, of course, only a dog man before I met Jeannie. I still am a dog man, and the only reason why Jeannie and I have never had a dog is that the cats of the household, Monty, Lama, Oliver and Ambrose, all hated dogs. On the other hand, although I may be fond of dogs, I am sometimes not so fond of their owners. Some of them inflict their dogs on other people without ever considering the annoyance, like perpetual barking, that such dogs can cause. Dogs have come to Minack who run riot, racing around the area, sniffing, making their marks, barking at the donkeys and chasing the cats. Poor things, they are only being their natural selves, so I do not blame them. I only blame their unimaginative owners who make remarks like: 'Fido isn't afraid of cats!' Or: 'He'll be all right with the donkeys . . . that bark doesn't mean anything . . .' and at that very moment Fred is prancing towards the dog, in anger, in readiness to bash it.

Fond as I am of dogs, therefore, I am on guard when one is in the neighbourhood; and so when Jeannie gave the collie the bone, I proceeded to shoo him away down the lane. I didn't want him hanging around, worrying Oliver and Ambrose, or Fred.

However, a couple of hours later he was back. I found him lying in the middle of the donkey field above the cottage, lying there quite still until he saw me approaching, and then he flicked his tail, hesitantly. Such shyness appealed to me. Here was a dog who, after receiving a luscious bone from a stranger, did not greedily return to the door. He had the subtle sense to keep out of sight, though no doubt longing to be noticed. He was noticed, and by me, and this meant I now became involved; and instead of shooing him away this time, I said to Jeannie that we must do everything possible to help him, and to find where he came from.

Jeannie proceeded to give him a name and, because it was Sunday, she called him Sunday. He was in admirable condition except for the mud on his coat; caked mud, which suggested he had been on the run for some length of time; and he also wore an old collar, and attached to the collar, about eighteen inches long, was a broken piece of nylon string. Obviously he had been tied up in a place he didn't like, and had bitten through the string to set himself free. I had a look at the collar to see if there was the owner's name on it, but could see nothing. This, as it later turned out, was a mistake on my part. However, at the time, we decided that the only thing I could do was to put Sunday in the car and, while Jeannie continued to bunch the daffodils, take him round the farms in the area in the hope that someone would recognise him.

I took him first to our friends John and Dora Phillips at Tregiffian, who love animals, the farm where Jeannie collects the eggs, a farm where the yard around the house and buildings has a traditional farm scene of geese, and wandering cats, a dog or two, cackling hens, and cock-a-doodle-do cockerels, and the eggs are laid in odd places, in a hedge, in a hay rick, and have to be searched for. John said he had never seen Sunday before, and then took the trouble to telephone round to other farmers, and they too were not able to help.

Off I went to the Eddys at Boleigh. Had a word too with Enoch Prowse next door, then on to a couple of farms at Tregadgewith, and then to Leslie Payne's Post Office at St Buryan, and back towards Minack via Sparnon, calling at farms on the way; and all the while Sunday sat beside me on the floor, his head resting on my knee close to the gear lever, looking up at me adoringly, like a Landseer picture. No one could help.

We left him in the Orlyt for the night, bracken bedding, water, and a bone in addition to a plateful of food; and next morning he greeted me as if he had known me all his life, as if he were asking that we should never let him leave. This attention was flattering, touched me in fact, but it did not stop me from thinking first of Sunday's owner, and the desperate worry he must be experiencing. But who could be the owner? It now seemed unlikely that he was local, for nobody I met had ever seen the dog before.

It was now that Margaret Smith came to the rescue. She arrived on Monday morning, bright and cheerful, ready to spend a day of daffodil picking, bent double among the rows of California, recounting as she did so details of her manifold weekend activities to Jeannie, when on her arrival I introduced her to Sunday. Practical Margaret bent down, took hold of Sunday's collar, looked at it closely, and pronounced that there was a faint scratching on the small name plate; and she then proceeded to identify a telephone exchange and number.

I wasted no time in putting Sunday into the car and hurrying up the lane with him, and along the main road to the telephone kiosk at Sheffield. The telephone exchange Margaret had identified was five miles on the far side of Penzance.

I rang the number, excitedly asked the lady who answered whether a black and white collie had been lost because I had such a collie within a few feet of where I was speaking from; and she replied in a well controlled tone that the collie hadn't been seen since the Saturday. I felt a little flattened that there had not been a greater emotional response, as there would have been from me and Jeannie if, for instance, we had lost Oliver; and some-one had suddenly informed us that Oliver had been found.

An hour or so after giving the news, the owner arrived in a car to collect Sunday, and Sunday went towards her and out of our life, wagging his tail. But I still do not know how it was that he arrived at Minack, a broken nylon string attached to his collar, and his home five miles the other side of Penzance. The owner at the time joked: 'He wanted to be in a book.'

And so he is.

I reached the lane by Monty's Leap and the dog was still barking in the copse. I now yelled at the top of my voice and a moment later there emerged from the under-growth a young foxhound, who saw me, and bolted up the lane. I had already half-guessed what he had been barking at. My half-guess was now confirmed.

At the top of the tallest of the elms was Oliver.

He was in a fix. As soon as he saw me he gingerly turned himself round on the slender branch where he was perched, put out a paw with the intention of balancing himself as he descended, lost his nerve, miaowed, and stayed on the branch.

I could see that it was a very difficult descent for him to make. He had reached his Everest and was stuck there. Clearly, having been chased by the foxhound, having been frightened out of his wits, he had raced up the tree without thought of the consequences; and if I hadn't been on the premises he could have been there for hours.

In any case, the rescue was going to be a difficult one to achieve. The elm concerned was a slender one, like a poplar, the upper branches were twig-like, and the spot from where Oliver looked down at me was out of reach of my ladder. The only way I could manage it was to put the ladder against the tree, Jeannie holding it firm, while I stood on the topmost rung, one hand on a twig-like branch balancing me, while the other hand stretched out and tried to clasp Oliver.

I proceeded to climb the ladder, Jeannie murmuring be careful, be careful, reached the top rung, stretched out my right arm, and only with my fingers was I able to touch Oliver's paw. He was out of reach, and there was nothing I could do. There was no branch I could put my foot on to bring me closer to him, and I just had to look up into his face, and watch him make a soundless miaow. He was going to be there forever unless he had the courage to claw his way the couple of feet down the tree which would bring him within my grasp. So I began to talk to him, and Jeannie called to him from below, and then we decided to leave him for a while to allow him to get his nerve back. He knew rescuers were at hand. He now had to make up his mind to co-operate.

This he did. I returned up the ladder a half an hour later and, as soon as he saw me, like an acrobat about to perform a difficult feat, he began to weave his head, to shuffle his front paws . . . and it was crystal clear that he was at last ready to take a risk. The risk came off. Head first, he clawed down the couple of feet from his perch, and landed on my shoulder; and from then on the descent was simple.

Obviously, after the reunion, he had to be rewarded; and it was a coincidence that Jeannie had just boiled a pound of coley. Apart from tinned food, Oliver and

Ambrose had fresh fish from Newlyn two or three times a week; and a particular favourite of Oliver's was coley.

Several months before, however, Oliver had lost a tooth and, as a result, we had asked our new vet from Penzance to come out and have a look at the remainder of his teeth; and the vet, who has a special way with small animals, said if it hadn't been for the character of Oliver, Oliver having such a wild streak in him, he would have advised us to bring him to the surgery where his teeth would have been cleaned.

As the vet suggested, this would have upset Oliver greatly, and it was part of the vet's sensitiveness that he did not press us to take him to the surgery; and he then agreed that we should experiment with an idea put to me by a reader who one day came down the winding lane.

The idea was very simple. To keep a cat's teeth white, mix puppy biscuits with all its food. Hence, long before Oliver's escapade, we had been mixing puppy biscuits with his and Ambrose's food; and the change in Oliver had been remarkable. His teeth were white, and he hadn't lost another; and both ourselves and the young vet were delighted. The biscuits, perhaps because of the vitamins contained therein, that were very special for growing puppies, also had another effect on him. Always talkative, after a few weeks he developed a new sound. It was a yap.

Meanwhile, I, in my role as Geoffrey's successor, was losing my temper with two of the machines I especially relied upon. Both of them, the small rotovator and the heavy, hand-steered grass and undergrowth motor mower, obstinately refused to start whenever I wanted to use them. The large Leyland tractor, however, was docile, and I had come to terms with it, and it had been invaluable during the daffodil season when I used to drive it out to the meadows and collect the baskets of picked daffodils. Indeed, when the daffodil season was over and we looked back upon it, we agreed that it had been the happiest daffodil season ever. It was not a particularly good one for prices, but then our outgoing expenses were much lower; and so we did not have the pressure to send daffodils away at the times when the price was particularly low, just because we needed the turnover to pay for the wages. When the price dipped, we stopped picking.

There were other factors to make the season a happy one, though these factors are constant every year. They involve the people with whom one associates during the progress of the season. It is refreshing to live in a setting where people, without self-conscious effort, help each other. This help does not necessarily come in a practical fashion. It comes in the form of enthusiasm or sympathy or cheerfulness, or the simple aim to be friendly. It exists at Penzance Station, where George Mills and other members of the railway staff greet us when we arrive late for the flower train, opening the rear door before I have stopped, ready to rush the boxes into the wagon, checking that my address labels are correct, good humouredly waving us goodbye and telling us not to be late next time. It exists at the headquarters of the Society of Growers, who organise the sales distribution of our daffodils, and it exists at Monro's, the horticultural sundries firm at Long Rock outside Penzance, where Ken and Des have looked after our needs for years. They reserve boxes of rubber bands for us, order the flower boxes in advance on our behalf when they think they are going to be in short supply, see that we have the metal strips which keep the packed daffodils in place in the box, and during the rest of the year advise us on the fertilisers to use and any other problem connected with growing.

They had advised me, for instance, not to use herbicide on the chickweed which grew at a pace in the carrot greenhouses even before a single carrot had germinated. I had been tempted to do so because my efforts to keep the ground moist, my patient hosing of every corner of each greenhouse, had only resulted in a carpet of chickweed. The chickweed revelled in my watering, the carrots

152

ignored it. The reasoning against the use of a herbicide, of course, was a sensible one. The herbicide, untouched by natural rain which would in time dilute it into oblivion, was likely to remain in the soil and so damage a following crop. A man he knew, said Des, lost ten thousand lettuces that way. Thus I had no alternative, Jeannie too, but to get down on hands and knees and pull up the chickweed, only to find a week later that it was covering the ground again.

The tomatoes, however, showed much promise. We had a puny number of plants compared with other years, one hundred and fifty instead of three thousand. We had planted them in the middle of March, no heat of course, and the variety, as before, was Maascross, a tomato with a fine flavour though not as large as other varieties, and with a minor disadvantage in that the gap between each truss is longer than usual. However, we had always found it a reliable tomato and, having so few, we would be able to look after the plants properly, and so obtain more pounds per plant than in previous years. We gave them extra space between plants, for instance, a space of two feet, in double rows also two feet apart; and after ball watering them in when planting, then waiting until the first flower on the first truss appeared, I proceeded to feed them every ten days with a dry fertiliser and water by hose every other day.

Jeannie was in charge of the pinching out of the side-shoots and, as the season progressed, of winding each plant around the string I had attached to the overhead wires. As for weeding, there was chickweed, as always, which had to be kept under control; and then later in the summer we had to cope with the rampant oxalis. Oxalis is advertised in some catalogues for sale at 50p for twenty-five bulbs, and that is the pink shamrock variety . . . but beware of the white and purple varieties, their leaves looking like handfuls of clover on the ground, because once you have had one of the tiny bulbs in your garden or greenhouse, you will never get rid of them. Our particular

tiny bulb, now ancestor of millions of others, came from a
market garden from which, at that time, we bought our
tomato plants. When it first appeared in flower I had no
idea of its menace; and the menace now ever increases.
Dig up weeds, old tomato plants, runner beans or peas,
and it's no use putting them on the compost heap. The
tiny bulbs, embedded in the roots, will continue to
multiply, and so ruin the compost.

The tomatoes only filled half of the hundred feet by
twenty feet Orlyt, and much of the other half provided a
fine example of Jeannie's inability to throw a plant away.
In this case, the plants were scarlet geraniums. A couple
of years ago she had heeled in a few geraniums at the side
of the greenhouse during the autumn, and did not transplant all of them into the garden the following spring.
Those that remained began to spread. They spread in such
profusion, filling this part of the greenhouse with such a
blaze of colour that no one who saw them could believe
that they were there by mistake.

There were also legions of geranium seedlings. Visitors
looked at them, asked for them, told her what a fortune
she could get from them if she sold them professionally,
but the seedlings remained. Jeannie would not sell. She
looked at them, expressed amazement that they should
be so prolific, praiseworthily put some of them in the
garden . . . and firmly refused to allow me to remove the
mass of them, and so make room for something more
useful.

She had, however, other reasons why they should
remain there. One reason was that in the autumn of the
previous year a frog had taken residence in the Orlyt; and,
as a child, she had believed a frog was a prince in disguise.
On this basis, therefore, the frog had to be protected and
allowed to wander at will in the Orlyt, and one of its
favourite spots was among the geraniums. As time went
by, other frogs took up residence and I dug a hole in the
ground and placed a basin in it, full of water for them to

swim in. Pandering to frogs is, of course, a foolish affair, but one has to remember that in many areas frogs have been obliterated from the natural scene; and so this whim of Jeannie's was not so silly as it might appear.

Their presence, however, inhibited my activities in the Orlyt. I could not weed because I had to leave cover for the frogs to hide in. I would pick up a hoe with the intention of having a bash at the oxalis or the bindweed, only to see a quiver in the foliage below me, then the hop of a frog. Thus my good intentions to keep the place tidy slowly evaporated, and although in one part of the top half I grew cucumbers and marrows for ourselves, the rest of it became a dumping ground for the fertiliser bags of the tomatoes, and a wire frame where I stored what was left of last year's onions, and seed boxes of flower plants for the garden, and branches of elder for rooting, and bracken for donkey bedding. Jeannie's mania for geraniums, you see, had had its effect on me. I too was behaving in an impractical manner.

Jeannie, however, had another impractical reason for the retention of her geraniums. Oliver and Ambrose had taken a liking to the top half of the Orlyt and its general untidiness and, so much was their liking for it, that Jeannie christened it the Cats Leisure Centre.

There were odd aspects to this Leisure Centre. One would have expected that Oliver and Ambrose would have treated it as their own, a sort of exclusive club in fact. Ambrose had a favourite spot between the end of Jeannie's geraniums, and the first of the Maascross tomato plants, a delightful place to sleep; and at other times both together would choose the donkey bracken, and they would curl there, paws around each other. During the day they would be in the Leisure Centre and at night I would leave the door ajar, and often they would sleep there, leaving me to stretch my legs in my own bed.

But the odd aspect of the Leisure Centre was that they showed no objection to the presence of others, such as the frogs. I have seen a frog hop past Ambrose within a foot of him, and he took no notice. I have seen Oliver stare at a frog. No reaction from him at all. Perhaps the oddest aspect of their behaviour in the Leisure Centre is that towards the blackbirds.

Blackbirds, you may know, are mad about tomatoes. Moreover, they are connoisseurs as to the quality and ripeness of tomatoes. I never, for instance, have seen a blackbird in a greenhouse until the tomatoes, the first truss that is, have begun to ripen. Then, through the ventilation vents and through the open doors, the blackbirds will appear, hopping up and down the rows, and flying up to any tomato which takes their fancy; and taking a juicy bite.

One would have thought we could have trusted Oliver and Ambrose to be guardians of these tomatoes. I would not have wished them to behave like security dogs, prowling round an empty factory and ready to pounce upon any intruder . . . but I would have expected that their very presence in the Orlyt would have scared the blackbirds away. This was not so. Ambrose would be resting in his favourite spot between the geraniums and the tomato plants while the blackbird would be gorging a tomato a couple of plants away, seemingly aware that he was immune from attack. Oliver's attitude was no different. I once saw a blackbird with half a tomato stuffed in his beak running up the greenhouse with the intention of taking it through the open door, and then perhaps to its young in the nest . . . but, as he was passing Oliver, he dropped it. Oliver raised his head from the bracken where he was lying, blinked, then idly watched the blackbird spoon it up in his bill, before setting off for the door again.

Thus the Leisure Centre was not only for cats. It was for frogs and blackbirds as well.

ELEVEN

'A donkey is advertised for sale in the *Cornishman*.'

The *Cornishman*, our admirable local newspaper, which circulates to Cornishmen around the world.

'Does it say where?' asked Jeannie.

'Zennor.'

'What else?'

'It is a prize winning stallion.'

'Oh no, that won't do. Fred wouldn't like a stallion.'

Fred being a gelding.

'That may be a problem, finding a donkey he likes.'

'We'll take our time.'

The drought, the long hot summer, had made me languid. I would spend hours transfixed by tranquillity, a mood which stopped me from performing anything of importance. I became immersed in idleness. I would stare and listen, and be absorbed in that other dimension of life which hurrying man seldom has the time to enjoy.

The chuckle of a green woodpecker, for instance, coming from the wood, a bee settling on a blackberry flower, a lizard sneaking out of a crevice in the wall beside the verbena bush, pedestals of pennywort miraculously growing in finger nail shallow earth, ants from summer's beginning to summer's end marching in single line round the cottage past the blue water butt and around towards the porch neatly taking a route that skirted the bottom of the front door, a persistent churring of a whitethroat among the brambles and bracken surrounding the well, the aroma of a distant moorland fire, a flycatcher with dumpy chest pausing on an ash branch then darting at a cabbage white, the ground hard and slippery as ice so that I kept Fred on a halter as I walked him along the cliff path, Monty's Leap dried up, the small reservoir empty, the well water only pumping twenty gallons a day, curlews flighting across the valley, settling on the dried grass field opposite, calling all the while their sad cries, Red Admirals on ivy leaves, white moths in the evening fluttering around the night scented stock and the mauve and white tobacco plants, Ronald the rook chortling on the roof, Philip the old gull astride the glass roof of the porch stamping at it with his beak, vexed that I had painted it with white shading, stopping him from looking down at us as we sat inside, far travelling bees humming among the escallonia, yachts in Mount's Bay resembling toy boats on a pond, Charlie the chaffinch gobbling Jeannie's coconut cake, Charlie busy with his own family but also, this being so strange, feeding a young robin.

Such peaceful idleness, however, did not mean that we were living in a lotus land all day. We had the alarm clock ringing in our ears at five in the morning; and while it was still cool we did our work. By breakfast time we had dug potatoes from greenhouse A, or pinched out the tomatoes, or picked them, or raked the hay into heaps, then piled it into the tractor, and carried it to the stack we built beside the winding lane. We pulled carrots too in the early morning, though it was only on three occasions we did this. Nobody wanted them. Last year a bonanza for carrot growers, this year the public had no wish for them. Probably it was because of the hot weather, but though we were disappointed we were consoled by the fact they had cost so little to grow. Nor did we have a bumper crop. They had grown in spasmodic patches, indeed many were still germinating; and so we had the satisfaction of knowing that there would be carrots galore for Fred during the winter, and for Fred's companion when he arrived.

A minor triumph concerned the potatoes. In the days of the first vision, potatoes dominated our lives. The delicious new potato. There was much competition in the area as to who was to be the first to draw the early potatoes, much gossip in the local pubs as to how this meadow or that was developing, and a bet or two, a pint being the prize, would be made. Perhaps Tom Laity would be first, or someone down at Mousehole . . . or Tangye. Tangye, the newcomer, had created early growing ground out of the cliff undergrowth. He was the unknown quantity, perhaps *he* would be the first to draw.

I wasn't. Instead I used to watch Tom Laity, and Joe Richards who shovelled for him, bringing up chip baskets of clean new potatoes from his cliff, then watch John, my immediate neighbour, doing the same, watch enviously, because I knew our own potatoes, because our meadows did not face exactly south as theirs did, were not ready. They were white, unripened, and they would cling to the plant when it was shaken, instead of freely dropping.

This year, the year of the hot summer, however, we had lush rows of early potatoes growing in greenhouse A by the middle of April, and by the beginning of May they were ready to draw. We had planted them at the beginning of February, Jeannie dropping the seed potato, Pilot was the variety, in the rows while I shovelled open the rows. We had carefully looked after them, kept them weeded, and watered them so that the soil was always damp, helping the potatoes to swell.

In the open, on the other hand, growers were having trouble. The plants were not growing. The potatoes growing on the plants were the size of marbles. All potato growers were praying for rain. Except Jeannie and me.

One happy May early morning, Jeannie and I dug our

first four, twelve pound chip baskets, beautiful clean potatoes, without a blemish, an achievement which deserved accolades. Hence when we had put them in the car, and I set off to take them to the salesman in Penzance, I had a special hope. One of my neighbours would see me. One of my neighbours would stop me for some reason, then catch sight of the earliest potatoes of anybody in the neighbourhood, and express astonishment.

Thus when I drove up the winding lane, up to the farm buildings at the top where I could expect to see Jack Cochram, or Bill Trevorrow, or Walter Grose, I drove very slowly. I drove so slowly past Bill Trevorrow's home that the engine stalled ... but nobody was to be seen. Here I was triumphant, and I and my potatoes were alone.

I carried on towards the main road, hoping that Jack or Bill or Walter had gone ahead of me for some reason, and that therefore I still had a chance of meeting one of them. On, on, I went, and not a soul did I see. Then at last I reached the main road, and turning right, I saw Enoch loping towards me, Enoch Prowse, friend since our beginning, who persuaded the donkeys with his epithets to walk round the corner towards Menwinnion, Enoch with the flowing white hair, and as soon as I saw him, I pulled to a stop.

'Hullo, Enoch,' I said casually.

'What do *you* want?'

Nothing offensive about that. I had stopped, and he wanted to know why.

'How are you feeling?'

'I'm all right,' he replied, puzzled.

'Lovely weather,' I said.

And as I said this, I made a cumbersome gesture of turning round in my seat, as if I was wanting to collect something in the back of the car.

'What have you got there?'

The question was like a stab.

Enoch had seen my potatoes.

'Early, they're early.'

'The first of anyone around here,' I said.

He grinned.

'You're a good farmer, you're a good farmer, no one can deny that.'

For a moment I felt genuinely flattered.

Then he winked.

'A good farmer, you are.'

June, July, August, September . . . people drifted down the winding lane.

'I don't want to intrude but . . .'

Sometimes I would be charging round a field with the motor mower, or Jeannie, in shorts, would be picking the tomatoes. Sometimes she would be bent double weeding the garden, or I would be powdered by the dust of the soil which I was rotovating. Sometimes we would be eating tomato and cucumber sandwiches for lunch on the bridge, sometimes Jeannie was about to serve dinner. Sometimes no one appeared for a couple of days. Sometimes several people in a single day.

'I don't want to intrude but . . .'

People would ask for books, and we would sign them, and when they brought out their money, I would say that Jeannie was the treasurer; and Jeannie would hurry back to the cottage to collect change. She would return, hand the change over . . . and there would be an embarrassed pause.

'Excuse me,' the purchaser would murmur, 'but I gave you a ten pound note, not a fiver.'

'Third time in a month she's made this mistake,' I would say, laughing. Poor Jeannie, she would fetch the correct change and hand it over in confusion.

People would commiserate with Fred as he stood beside the wrought iron gate above the cottage, stroking him, giving him carrots; and they would ask to see Oliver and Ambrose.

'Do you know where they are?' I would call out to Jeannie.

'They were on the garage roof a short while ago.'

I would look, and they would not be there.

Five minutes, ten, fifteen, and the fruitless, irritating search would continue. Not a sign of them.

'Perhaps next time we'll be lucky,' the people would say as they left.

'I don't want to intrude but . . .'

I would listen. Fragments of conversation I would remember:

'I had a good job in a London hospital and I was very happy there,' said a young electrician who came down the winding lane, 'but it took me three hours to travel there and back every day . . . and I suddenly realised I was wasting three hours every day of my life. So I've found a job in a hospital near home . . . I've lost £7 a week but I've gained fifteen hours a week with my family.'

'I heard Malcolm Muggeridge on a programme the other evening referring to the banality of truth,' said a clergyman from Bristol, incensed, '. . . what nonsense! If that was so, Christ's teachings are banal.'

'I was terrified of snakes, terrified of them. Then my husband slowly persuaded me to change my mind. Now I have them weaving about in our sitting room.' The husband interrupted: 'You've adders around here . . . I can give you a tip about them. Adders have weak muscles. Hold an adder up by its tail, and it won't have the strength to twist and bite you.'

A young man, making signs, then taking a notebook from his pocket, and scribbling a message: 'I'm deaf and dumb. I live at St Albans and staying at Falmouth . . . I hear sounds in your books.'

'I hate you, Mr Tangye,' said the large man jocularly, a tycoon farmer from up country who was buying up small farms in the area, bulldozing the hedges and making small fields into prairie fields, 'because my wife keeps reading to me from your books about the crop disasters that have happened to you, saying I have made a mistake coming to Cornwall, and they will happen to me '

They did.

'My uncle,' said the young German, 'was the head of a big combine. On the day of his retirement he said: "I've got everything I have worked for, house, money, fame . . . but I was wrong. I should have worked to gain happiness." '

An old farmer of the district arrived with his grand-daughter who wanted to meet Fred and who lived in London: 'She won't get me to London . . . she wouldn' get me there if she gave me a cow and a calf.'

Out of a car stepped four ladies from the Midlands:

'Look at those two gulls on the roof,' says one, 'they can't be real.'

'No,' I reply, 'they're made of plastic.'

'I thought so.'

A pause.

'Look, Cherry! They're moving!'

A young American couple, on a month's holiday from the States, arrive to take photographs of Oliver and Ambrose: 'Twice a week we call home in San Francisco to find out how the cats are.'

A woman in great distress: 'I've lost my Siamese! I brought it on holiday with me from Luton, and it disappeared from our caravan a week ago. We have searched every field within five miles radius . . . and I have to go home tomorrow!'

This Siamese was found six months later by a farmer in an unused barn . . . fit and well.

A French priest who drove here from his village on the Loire by way of the Roscoff–Plymouth Ferry, spending the morning wandering around: 'C'est paradis . . . a place where one can pray.'

The priest had walked to Carn Barges, and had sat there staring at the sea. Sometimes people who call like to make the same walk, and we show them the white gate into Fred's field where they join the coastal path, the official path which now runs round Cornwall. There is, of course, no public path through Minack. Yet, periodically, a busybody or two seek to obtain such a public path. One can imagine what would happen if they succeeded . . . dogs chasing Oliver and Ambrose, donkeys chasing the dogs, and strangers able to pass by, day and night, within a few yards of our windows. Hence, although we welcome the sincere, we are on the alert for the busybodies. The busybodies only look for trouble.

The truth is that this question of public footpaths exemplifies a basic difference between the urban mind and the countryman's mind. The urban mind views the country-side as a vast park with all the streamlined facilities that a park should provide . . . easily walked paths, clearly signposted, and plenty of them to satisfy the whim of anyone in the mood to use one. To obtain the right of way on these paths, however, methods are adopted which are sometimes objectionable to a countryman.

A footpath society or a rambler association, for instance, will set out to prove that the path in question was in use distant years gone by, and they will search out old people to prove it. This may sound sensible enough, until one realises the difference between today's users of such a path and the users of long ago. In the old days the path had a functional purpose . . . the postman walked it, a farm labourer walked to the farm where he worked, or it was the means of contact between neighbours. Thus, as it was an age when strangers were few and far between, it did not matter that the path passed within a few feet of a farm or a cottage. Nor did it matter if it went across the middle of a field because the user, in those days, would instinc-tively walk round the field and not across it if the field was being cropped.

Today, however, a different kind of person uses the paths; and instead of the local user of the past, there may

166

be a tramping pack of people marching along. Hence it is absurd to claim ancient paths as the legal highways of today. Times have changed.

Of course footpaths are an essential part of the environment today but they should be mapped with due regard to the privacy and convenience of the countryman who, after all, is paying the rates on the land, and who is earning his living from the land. There is, too, an attitude on the part of some members of footpath societies and rambler associations to which the countryman objects, a bossy superiority which grates. This touchiness on the part of the countryman I can understand because, before I came to live at Minack, I too had an urban mind. My behaviour when I first came, I realise in retrospect, was quite often out of tune with those whose families had lived in the area for generations. I was impatient with their slow ways. I had the urban wish for instant results. I *felt* superior. But at least Jeannie and I had come to stay, and had time to learn that our urban standards were wrong.

No one can complain, however, about the creation of the coastal path, and I have special reason to be grateful for its official presence. I used to keep the path clear of undergrowth myself between our boundary and Carn Barges and beyond, bashing at the brambles with a slasher, donkeys behind me, a donkey nose sometimes pushed into my back to hurry me on, but I have no longer this laborious work to do. Twice a year council workmen do the work instead. A pleasant wide path, easy for everyone to walk along.

But there are snags, and litter as usual is one of them. The urban attitude of treating the countryside as a dustbin has always been a mystery to me. People do not leave debris on the lawns of their gardens, or on the carpet of their sitting rooms, so why do they behave as they do when they visit the countryside? Paper tissues, for instance. are a menace. Sometimes I have walked along the coastal path, and I might have been taking part in a paper chase. Why cannot tissue users hide the tissues in the undergrowth instead of dropping them on the path for all to see? And if walkers are eating sweets and chocolate why do they have to drop the wrappings on the path?

Incidentally, if you ever meet a donkey when you are out walking, never feed it with meat, such as a left-over sandwich. Meat kills a donkey, just as plastic wrappings might kill.

Some walkers seem to become enraged at the sight of signposts. Official wooden signposts on the coastal path are periodically smashed to satisfy someone's aggro emotions of the moment. Across our land we have path notices of our own making and these also are sometimes torn up from the ground and flung away into the under-growth. What prompts a walker to do this? Not only walkers, however, vandalise our footpath notices. The other day I came through the white gate, observed that one of the notices was missing, cursed the unknown walker, then saw to my left, galloping around in the grass, a black labrador. In his mouth, the path notice.

Jeannie, when I told her, laughed, because a black labrador figures in the folk history of her family. Her father, Frank Nicol, was an officer in the London Scottish during the First World War and was badly gassed. He suffered chest problems for the rest of his life, though he never bored anyone with his suffering. He was a gregarious man, with lots of friends at the golf club of St Albans where the family lived, lots of friends everywhere including London where he had built up a rating surveyor's business representing many well-known firms, and at East Mersea where the family had a holiday cottage.

When I came along he was naturally suspicious. He was meeting at last the problem which fathers, and mothers, sometimes hesitate to face. The daughter is about to fly away; the bringing up, the education, the term holidays, the sacrifice in money terms, and the story is over. I was, however, insensitive to his feelings at the time because he was so endearing.

'What will you have?' he would ask as we sat at the bar, at the time he knew he was losing Jeannie. Then turning to the barman: 'Make it a double.'

In his wish for other people to be happy, he was unnecessarily generous, and often at his family's expense. He sold Bryher Lodge, the house he had built to his own design at St Albans, for a song, because he liked the face of the purchaser. Similarly he sold the house at East Mersea which he had also built to his own design. He was a delightful companion, often very funny, never a moaner despite his health, and a living example of what I had always imagined was the best in the Old Contemptibles.

The story of the black labrador concerned his return one afternoon from the Verulam Golf Club near St Albans. He was driving an Armstrong Siddeley, a notable car of the time, and much prized by the family. At the entrance to Bryher Lodge was a magnificent pair of wrought iron gates and, that afternoon, on turning off the road, Frank Nicol hit one of them.

A little while later Jeannie and her sister Barbara saw the damage to the car. They cried out: 'What happened, Daddy? How did the car get so damaged?'

'It was a black labrador,' replied their father gruffly, 'it ran across the drive and I had to swerve.'

Forever afterwards when one of them was in trouble at home she would explain: 'It was a black labrador, Daddy, that got me into trouble.'

At daffodil time we have to keep a special watch on the coastal path. Walkers are scarce at that time of the year, and those who follow the path usually do so because they wish to indulge in the glory of seeing the daffodils in February and March. There are, however, occasional exceptions, and the exceptions are those who sneak along the path picking the daffodils from the meadows on either side, and which we ourselves would have sent to market, or just left there for everyone to enjoy as they passed by. It is very rare to catch the culprits in the act, but this season, the season when Fred took a liking to Margaret's woollen hat, I did so.

Soon after breakfast Jeannie and I had taken a couple of baskets down the onion cliff, and slowly worked our way up from meadow to meadow, picking the Magnificence we grew there. Having filled the baskets we began our way back to the cottage, following the coastal path. There is a shallow turn in this path which hides from view our other meadows, and it was when we passed this turn that I saw a hundred yards away, bending down, picking quickly like professional pickers, a man and a woman.

'Leave this to me,' I said to Jeannie, my adrenalin rising.

I walked on, and the man and the woman continued to pick. They were elderly, the man large, the woman wispy, and as I approached they remained bent double, their backs to me. My footsteps were silent on the grass path, and I was able to come within a few yards of them before I asked, in a gentle voice:

'Can I help?'

They both shot up. The woman half fell into a gorse bush protruding from the hedge, and the man nearly tripped into the vast paper bag which contained the daffodils he had already picked.

'We're picking daffodils.'

'So I see.'

'Just a few.'

'A few too many,' I said, 'hand over to me what you've picked, and hop it.'

I had seen neither of them before.

'And what's more,' I added, 'I now see that you have been picking green buds.'

'They'll bloom later,' said the man.

'Not in your house,' I replied.

The woman had already gone, sidling past Jeannie, then running away towards Tater-du lighthouse.

'Come on,' I said to the man, 'give them to me.'

And he reluctantly did so.

I seldom lock the white gate. I may do so if we are going away for the day and occasionally, when I see a busybody in the area, I will hurry down and put the padlock on it. One day in the summer, I saw such a busybody, and proceeded to lock the gate, little realising the predicament in which this act was going to put me.

That night, it was a still one, Jeannie and I were woken up by the dazzling light of a flare beaming into the bedroom, and then we heard the distant sound of the maroons being fired from the lifeboat station at Mousehole. Presumably some boat was in distress despite the clear night, despite the still sea, or some mystery accident had occurred. We put on dressing gowns, and went outside where the garden looked as if an arc lamp was lighting it up. Suddenly we heard voices. We listened.

'They are coming from below Carn Barges,' Jeannie said excitedly.

There was no doubt about it. Here it was one o'clock in the morning, a flare overhead, maroons, and voices on the rocks. A boat must have come aground.

'Let's hurry,' I said . . . and we both set off, running down the path to the white gate.

I had, however, forgotten that I had locked it.

'Damn,' I said, when we reached it.

It was an awkwardly designed gate, unlike the normal field gate, and certainly not easy to climb over. Moreover at the left end of the gate, the hinges end, were the prickly branches of a blackthorn, and at the right end, the padlock end, a bank of grass, dried up bracken, and brambles.

'There's not a moment to lose,' said Jeannie, in gear to the challenge of rescuing the foundered sailors, 'help me over.'

I had no difficulty in doing so. I lifted her up on to the bank, kept her dressing gown free from the gate, and a moment later she was running down the coastal path towards the sound of the voices.

I now had to follow her, but there was no one to lift me up to the bank. I started to flounder, grasping grass and bracken, heaving myself up, then falling back as the grass and bracken broke in my grasp.

It was now that Fred appeared. Obviously he had been up in the Q.E.2 field when we had first run down the path, and he hadn't immediately responded to the potential excitement. He was now most certainly aware of this excitement, and, while I struggled to climb over the gate, he shouted his awareness into the silent night by a series of hee-haws.

This didn't help me. I now had struggled three quarters of the way up the bank, but part of my dressing gown had become caught on some part of the gate, and another part had become entwined in the brambles. Thus I was jammed, spread-eagled half over the gate, half on the bank, with Fred hooting at my bare leg level.

'Help!' I called out to Jeannie.

Jeannie was out of sight. She had run on down the coastal path towards the sound of the voices, and so there I was poised in isolation on top of a gate with a donkey below me hooting his head off.

A minute later Jeannie was back, disentangled my dressing gown, and I was free. She had also traced the source of the voices. No boat. Only night fishermen fishing from the rocks. And next morning we learnt that the flare and the maroons were the result of a false alarm. Our excitement, therefore, Fred's excitement, was quite unnecessary. But we have a souvenir of the occasion.

On going into the orchard in the morning I found hanging from an apple tree, a small white parachute. The parachute of the flare.

We had by now become determined to find a friend for Fred. I had continued to look out for advertisements in the local papers, but no one was in the mood to sell a donkey. The matter was becoming urgent because the long nights were setting in, and the prospect of Fred being on his own as the rains fell and the gales blew was not one that we could bear. He had attention, endless attention during the summer, but now he would be spending many hours by himself. We could not allow this to happen.

One day we set off to find Roy Teague, the Roy Teague who sold us Penny, who, at the time, kept the Plume of Feathers at Scorrier. Roy Teague still lived in the district, still dealt in donkeys and horses, and we thought it nostalgically appropriate if the man who provided us with Penny could provide us with Penny's successor.

It was, however, to prove a fruitless search. We first called at the Plume of Feathers to discover his address. The pub now stands isolated, a few hundred yards away from the Redruth by-pass, and half the field where Penny stood when we first saw her, is buried in concrete. The pub inside is still the same, old world, charming, but we sensed a desolation which was not there when Roy Teague reigned behind the bar. Or perhaps it was just because we were remembering that time years ago when we stood there, glasses in hand, the Land Rover outside, buying a donkey which we had never expected to buy. Perhaps it was the spent years with Penny we were remembering, and which caused our sense of desolation.

We were given Roy Teague's address, went to it, and he was not there. He was at Helston market, we were told, and off we went to Helston market. We wandered among the farmers as they called out their bids at the auction, asking if anyone had seen Roy Teague, being told that he had been seen five minutes before, but still not finding him. At last we gave up the search, and drove home; and Jeannie, who has faith in such matters, said it was meant that we should not find him.

A week later I picked up the Donkey Breed Society News Letter, and I was looking through its roneoed paragraphs when I saw one which caused me to call out to Jeannie: 'We've found him!'

Under the heading 'Donkeys For Sale' was the following:

MINGOOSE MERLIN, large dark brown 18 months old registered gelding, by ROMANY OF HUNTERS BROOK, ex prize-winning mare. Very successfully shown, excellent potential for driving. Kind, knowledgeable home for this exceptionally handsome and lovable donkey my first consideration. Mrs. V. Bailey, The Forge, Skinners Bottom, Redruth, Cornwall.

'And he comes from Penny land!' said Jeannie.

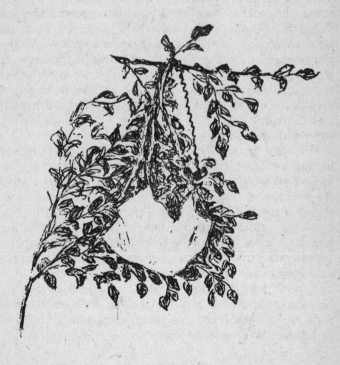

TWELVE

We met Mingoose Merlin over a fence at Skinners Bottom the following afternoon. We were not going to allow ourselves to change our minds, to dither. Fred had waited long enough for a companion. As we set off from Minack we had agreed that Mingoose Merlin was going to be ours.

I had, however, never acquired an animal from a private home before, a pet which had to be sold for reasons beyond the control of the owner; and when I met the young couple who were waiting for us, after the telephone call I had made to say we were on our way, I suddenly felt like an interloper. Here I was, cheque book in my pocket, about to take out of their lives a pet they loved. Penny, when we bought her, was wanting a home. Mingoose Merlin had one.

But there was a special reason why Mingoose Merlin had to go, and the couple explained it to us. They were a delightful couple. The girl came from London, and her husband from Jamaica, and both of them had that emotional attitude to animals of which logical people disapprove. Des Bailey came from Jamaica to train at a London hospital as an anaesthetic technician but his real interest concerned animals, horses in particular, and after his marriage to Val they made an astonishing decision. They would leave London to live in Cornwall, and he would become a farrier. He is now a travelling farrier, and he attends horses and donkeys in all parts of the county.

They had bought Mingoose Merlin from a donkey breeder nearby, Jennifer Hillyard, who later told us that Mingoose Merlin was the most lovable donkey she had ever bred. But, because of her other donkeys she had no room for him, and hence she sold him to Des and Val Bailey. We also learnt that Mingoose was the village where she had her stud farm, and that the name Mingoose Merlin was chosen as being a dignified name for his entry into the Donkey Society Stud Book. Mingoose Merlin, however, was Merlin to his friends.

Merlin was now being sold by the Baileys because they had another donkey, an old donkey of whom they were particularly fond, and who had recently had an operation. Merlin, they realised, was too rumbustious to be a companion to a sick donkey, and so they reluctantly decided to find another home for him.

On hearing this explanation I was coolly practical. We were going to buy Merlin, that was for sure, despite the fact we had yet to meet him but, bearing in mind the possibility that Fred might take an instant dislike to him, might take exception to his rumbustious behaviour, I asked if Merlin could come on a week's approval.

'You see,' I explained, 'we are not buying him for ourselves. We are buying him for Fred.'

This was agreed, and we proceeded from the house to be introduced.

'Merlin!'

And Merlin appeared.

He bounced up to the fence like a dog wagging its tail, pushed his nose into my hand, then into Jeannie's, and skedaddled away out of sight round a farm building.

'Merlin!' Val Bailey called out again, anxiously, like a mother wanting a child to be on its best behaviour. 'Merlin!'

Merlin had a mind of his own. He had other things to do. But we had seen enough. Fred's coat had been short from the beginning. Merlin's brown coat was long, and Jeannie, laughing, said that he looked like a yak. The coat half covered his face, and it covered his legs so that he looked as if he was wearing plus fours.

'Yes,' I said, 'we'll have him.'

It was a Monday, and it was agreed that he would be brought to Minack in a horsebox on Wednesday morning. Merlin had had experience of horseboxes. He had been a Show donkey, third in the foal class of the Bath and West, best foal at six weeks in the Penzance Show, best foal at the Devon County Show, and sixth at the prestigious Stoneleigh Show. This latter placing must have been a blow to his pride. He had never been shown again.

So that Monday we hurried back and told Fred that he was soon to have a companion . . . and then I found, Jeannie found too, that despite our practical manner, we were excited. Wednesday was going to prove to be another milestone in our life at Minack.

But on the Tuesday we had other matters to occupy us. A storm force south westerly gale had blown up during the night, and by ten in the morning when the postman arrived, two large panes of glass in the Orlyt had been smashed. The gale raged all day, and not until evening was there a pause, a sudden silence among the trees, but then it began to rage again, and this time it came from due west.

The two smashed panes were on the side of the Orlyt, and I was able to plug them temporarily with polythene sheets. My main anxiety, as always, was that the roof panes of the greenhouses might be smashed, and then I would be powerless. Even in still weather it was a hazardous task to cope with repairs on the roof, in a gale it would be suicidal. I could only wait and hope, as I had done many times before when the gales blew.

There were, however, compensations. We had no

outside crops to worry about. We had no meadows of violets whose leaves would be whitened by the wind, or anemones whose stems would be broken. We had no meadows of early potatoes waiting to be obliterated by the gale. Only man-made glass was our concern.

Merlin, therefore, was for the moment forgotten; and in between staring impotently at the greenhouses, and looking out to sea at the ships coming into Mount's Bay for shelter, I wrote up my diary, not a social diary, but the diary of our labouring activities.

'Jeannie,' I said, when I had finished, 'I'm rather impressed with ourselves.'

'Tell me.'

'Not an hour of paid labour, and just look what we've done.'

'Due to my tractor driving,' she said, joking.

Jeannie had pursued me with her wish to learn to drive the tractor, but I had been loth to let her do so because I myself had also been learning to drive it. I was aware of the tractor tricks, and I didn't want both of us risking trouble. I had found that I had to keep cool to start it . . . push a gear into the slot marked S, push a lever on the dashboard which, when pulled out stopped the engine, push another gear into one of the slots marked High, Medium or Low; and then, after starting the engine, I had to take the gear out of S, and put it into slots One, Two, or Three. My mind, therefore, had to concentrate on two sets of gears and if, as I did once, I pushed one set of gears into slot Three, and the other set into slot High, then released the clutch and the footbrake, the tractor shot off like a bullet.

Jeannie was never that careless. Her fault was that she was forgetful about releasing the footbrake, which had to be done with a bang of the foot, and forgetful also about raising the lever which lifted the steel carrier box of the tractor. This box was the purpose of her driving the tractor I filled the box with the debris, such as the old tomato plants, and she drove the tractor to the dumping spot. Often, however, there would be a horrible grating noise as she moved off. She had forgotten to use the hydraulic lever to lift the box from the ground.

We were together in these matters, as we had been in the beginning. Our relationship had never been determined by conventional standards. We had always believed in living dangerously, undeterred by passing fancies, because we both knew the base was true. Marriage can become dull if the rules are obeyed. Marriage, a successful marriage, must never be allowed to quell the illusion of freedom. Marriage must be a love affair.

'The list of our achievements,' I went on, 'includes all those things I never believed we could do on our own . . . tomatoes cleared, Minack cliff cut down, onion cliff cut down, donkey field mowed, Q.E.2 field mowed, all the other daffodil meadows mowed or cut down, and the lane, both sides cut back, and the ditch cleared.'

'We must celebrate!'

'Not while this gale is blowing.'

The secret of our success lay in two machines I had bought. They were seemingly expensive but I consoled myself when I bought them by saying about one of them, 'that's three weeks' wages', and about another, 'that's five weeks' wages.' The wages I would have seen no more of. The machines remained.

The first machine I bought was an electric hedgecutter driven off a battery. A long lead connected the two, and the pattern of work was for me to carry the battery in a potato basket to the appointed spot, connect the lead, merrily cut away until the lead was at full stretch, then bring the battery to the spot I had reached, and cut away again. The task required concentration. Apart from any dangers from the cutter blades, there was another hazard to watch out for. I was warned about it when I bought the machine. Each time I took the machine out I reminded myself of the warning. Yet twice in the first two weeks of its use, I fell into the trap of forgetting. It was simply that the lead could become entangled in the undergrowth that I was cutting; and at the moment I snipped a choice patch of bracken, I also snipped the lead.

The second machine was a Brush Cutter, or that was the name given to it by the importers, for it came from Japan and the instructions were in Japanese. It was a dangerous looking machine. It was five feet long with an engine at one end, and a fiercesome circular blade at the other. Harness was attached to the machine which I arranged over my shoulders, and the engine, an easy to start engine, proceeded to whirl the circular blade around at speed while I swung the machine to and fro, as if I was using an old Father Time scythe.

On first being shown the machine, I expressed serious doubts about its safety. Supposing the blade became disconnected and flew off? Supposing the harness broke? Supposing this and that? I trundled out my doubts to the salesman who listened politely, saying nothing until I had run out of my imaginary fears. Then, as if he was delivering a karate chop, he said:

'The Mother Superior of our local convent has been using it all summer herself. She's had no trouble.'

If a Mother Superior could use it, so could I; and so as a result of that recommendation I bought the machine, and I now share the Mother Superior's enthusiasm. I too have not experienced any trouble. How the Mother Superior manages to operate it when wearing her customary habit I do not know. It is a demanding machine. It requires freedom of movement, and a strong back. After an hour or two of swinging to and fro, I myself am prepared to pack up for the morning.

But without its presence Jeannie and I would have been looking around Minack in dismay. The onion cliff for instance . . . when Geoffrey left I said to myself that the onion cliff was now finished, it would be quite impossible for me to clear it, clear all the meadows which sloped down the cliff like terraces of a vineyard, and I would have to leave it to become bramble covered, gorse covered, bracken covered, as it was a century or two ago before a crofter created it into meadows of production. Yet here we were at the beginning of November, and thanks to the Mother Superior, the meadows were cleared. Within three months daffodils would be picked.

It was the same with the Minack cliff meadows. I had begun clearing them before discovering the Japanese machine, using the hedgecutter, but the hedgecutter was unable to cut the dense tufts of couch grass which covered the meadows. It cut brambles and bracken, anything which its blades could bite, but it failed to do the complete task I wanted it to do. The day I put on the harness of the Mother Superior's machine, my life changed.

I took ten hours on different days to cut the meadows, and it used to take Geoffrey over a week to do so; and after the cutting Jeannie would be there to help pull the cut bracken, couch grass and brambles away, stacking them on the edge of the meadows. We would then both stand and admire a cleared meadow, and once I said to Jeannie: 'Why does it give us so much pleasure? After all in terms of money there's little in it.'

'We see the evidence that we are individuals,' she replied.

'Symbolic evidence.'

'Think of all those millions who never see the final results of their efforts, cogs in the computer age, no wonder they become frustrated.'

'And strike out of boredom.'

'Probably.'

'So that the pleasure that we have in looking at a cleared meadow is proof that we are free . . . as free as when we first came here.'

'That's what I mean,' said Jeannie.

'It's funny.'

'Why?'

'Civilisation's progress,' I answered, 'we are being so endlessly brainwashed into believing that a group society is the only way of living that you and I have to look at a meadow on a Cornish cliff to remind ourselves that we are still individuals.'

'We're lucky to have the chance.'

'Lucky too to feel the same way as we did in the beginning.'

Nothing fundamental has changed since the beginning. The rocks remain, fishing boats sail past offshore though more silent and faster, everywhere there are yellow flickers of November gorse, the sun glints on rain-wet ivy leaves, gulls float like snowflakes against the brown-red bracken of Carn Barges, a raven grunts overhead, his November courting having begun, a woodcock zig-zags, there is the thump of a wave on a rock sounding like the slamming of a door, hartstongue ferns peer green from banks, seaweed scents, foot wide tramped tracks of foxes trace through the meadows, cormorants on Gazelle Point air their wings . . .

Stay still, I say to myself, stay still and make the small kingdom your own. The hustlers see it all in a blur, blind to its activities, deaf too, hurrying onward out of boredom, and out of fear of meeting themselves.

'To know the whole process, the totality of oneself,' wrote Krishnamurti in *The First and Last Freedom*, 'does not require any expert, any authority. The pursuit of authority only breeds fear. No expert, no specialist, can show us to understand the process of self.'

Stay still, and I see the microscopic details of the kingdom. Stay still, and I am aware of the sounds that I haven't heard before, of the movement of insects that I haven't seen before, and of the wonder in the world that awaits our attention without relevance to the pay packet, or one upmanship, or the greed for power. Stay still, and I can become aware of my secret self, difficult though it may be. Groups do not give one a chance to do so. Groups, in their gatherings, chatter, postulate theories and solutions, but their members are only running away from themselves. Yet how can one blame them? People require comfort, and group minded people find this comfort together, particularly in cities where the pace, and the multitudes, deny them solitude; for loneliness is not the same as solitude.

The lane was not as difficult to cut back as the cliff meadows. I was not confined in a small space. I was able to swing the Japanese machine up and down, cutting away the nettles, the brambles, the couch grass, the bracken, as I did so. Yet I had always been scared about this trimming of the lane. I had not believed I was fitted to do so, that only a man who was brought up to do such work, was capable of doing it. A left-over of my urban mind.

It was different when we opened it up, when Jeannie and I, in the year of the first vision, took upon tasks that were only achieved with the help of unthinking enthusiasm. I then bought a sickle for Jeannie and a long-handled slasher for myself, and the two of us, that magical summer, opened up the winding lane to Minack. I have a photograph of us at work. Jeannie, very pretty in shorts, long dark hair over her shoulders (the great Cochran once tried to lure her from the Savoy to join his chorus line), and myself slashing away, looking as thin as a scarecrow.

Now here we were again having the satisfaction of working together at the entrance to Minack. But Jeannie didn't have a sickle in her hand this time, she was driving the tractor, and she was collecting the nettles, the couch grass, the bracken, the bramble, and piling them into the steel carrier box, then when this undergrowth was head high behind her as she sat on the tractor seat, a kind of wobbly haywain, she drove the tractor to the gap before Monty's Leap, then backed the tractor into it, and waited for me to unload it. I was always amazed when I did so what strength was required to lift the cut undergrowth with the long-handled fork out of the carrier box; and therefore what strength had been required to put it there

When the lane had been cleared, when the ditch had been spooned out with a shovel, when I had chipped shallow slits across the lane to catch the rain, leading the rain to the ditch, we indulged again in a moment of self-admiration. But this time we were in the company of Oliver and Ambrose.

It was a routine stroll. Oliver and Ambrose like to meander up the lane with us after they have had their breakfast, and before we have had our own. It is a slow stroll, and Jeannie calls it an H.A. which is short for hang about. It is at its slowest when we are going up the lane for our companions believe in taking their time, a pause at one tuft of grass, a false alert by the patch of violets just short of Monty's Leap, and then a magical moment when Oliver has a drink from the stream, or Ambrose takes a leap across it. Time is then telescoped . . . Lama is drinking, Monty is leaping.

We did not go far up the lane, just a quarter of the way up, short of the hidden well on the right, and then we stopped, and we metaphorically patted each other on the back. Strange too how proud we felt, as if we had won a prize at school.

As always our return was a quicker affair. Our companions scampered ahead, Oliver with tail up, and Ambrose beside him, down the winding lane to home.

It was also as if Mingoose Merlin was coming home, that Wednesday morning when he emerged from the horsebox which deposited him outside the farm buildings at the top of the hill. The gale had died away, the sun was shining, and there was the illusion of a soft spring day. He emerged from the horsebox meekly enough, and, after a momentary pause when he was presented with a carrot, Jeannie took hold of the halter and started to lead him down the winding lane to Minack.

They had gone but a few yards when he began to lead

her. His trot became faster and faster. She held him all right, but there was no doubt at all that he was in a great hurry. Round one bend, then another, then the straight run to Monty's Leap, and when he reached it, instead of walking through it, he jumped, plus fours in the air, shaggy coat flying, and, racing up the side of the barn with Jeannie running beside him, he turned left without hesitation.

And there, waiting at the gate, was Fred.

A SELECTION OF BESTSELLERS FROM SPHERE

FICTION

THE WATCHDOGS OF ABADDON	Ib Melchior £1.75	☐
EXPECTING MIRACLES	Linda Howard £1.50	☐
I, SAID THE SPY	Derek Lambert £1.75	☐
HEART OF WAR	John Masters £1.95	☐

FILM & TV TIE-INS

THE PROFESSIONALS 9 & 10	Ken Blake £1.00	☐
GOODBYE DARLING	James Mitchell 95p	☐
OUTLAND	Alan Dean Foster £1.50	☐
FORT APACHE, THE BRONX	Heywood Gould £1.75	☐

NON-FICTION

EMMA VIP	Sheila Hocken £1.25	☐
A WAY TO DIE	Rosemary & Victor Zorza £1.50	☐
MARY	Patricia Collins £1.50	☐
EAGLE DAY	Richard Collier £4.75	☐
WILL	G. Gordon Liddy £1.75	☐

All Sphere books are available at your local bookshop or newsagent, or can be ordered direct from the publisher. Just tick the titles you want and fill in the form below.

_____

Name _____

Address _____

_____

Write to Sphere Books, Cash Sales Department, PO Box 11, Falmouth, Cornwall TR10 9EN

Please enclose a cheque or postal order to the value of the cover price plus:

UK: 40p for the first book, 18p for the second book and 13p for each additional book ordered to a maximum charge of £1.49.

OVERSEAS: 60p for the first book plus 18p per copy for each additional book.

BFPO & EIRE: 40p for the first book, 18p for the second book plus 13p per copy for the next 7 books, thereafter 7p per book.

Sphere Books reserve the right to show new retail prices on covers which may differ from those previously advertised in the text or elsewhere, and to increase postal rates in accordance with the PO.